Succeeding in America

Lessons from Immigrants Who Achieved the American Dream

Succeeding in America

TeamCom Books
Silver Spring, MD
www.TeamComBooks.com
301-847-7600; 301-847-7638 (fax)

Credits

Lead Editor: Bruce Fries
Contributing Editors: Cheryl Hoffman, Ron Kenner,
Karen Porterfield and Chris Roerden
Cover Design: Michael Lynch
Author's Photo: Sharon Hopkins Kelly

Notice of Rights

Publisher's Cataloging-in-Publication Data

Gallares-Japzon, Leticia

Succeeding in America / lessons from immigrants who achieved the American dream / Leticia Gallares-Japzon — 1st ed.

p. cm.

Includes bibliographical references and index.

LCCN: 00-134739
ISBN: 1-928791-20-4

1. Success. 2. Immigrants—United States. 3. United States—Immigration. 4. United States—Social life and customs. 5. Assimilation (Sociology). I. Title.

JV6475.G35 2001 304.8'73

Printed and bound in the United States of America 9 8 7 6 5 4 3 2 1

To all immigrants and would-be immigrants,
may you find the lessons valuable, the
strategies useful, and the stories inspiring.

Acknowledgments

Special thanks go to many people, most especially the following:

Once-upon-a-time immigrants who contributed to this book—Christina Bonnell, Louis Cheng, Mike Ghanna, Georg Hirsch, Maria Jaramillo, Dave Lang, Ellen Dimaano Latham, Elena Minnitti, Bella Morin, Chung K. Pak, Sam Quaye, Nilofer Qureshi, Bharat Sahay, Ravi Sahay, Julio Sasaki, Liklik Schroeder, Lina Shoobridge, Evelyn Shu, William Skea, Nora Szeto, Henry Tse, Gabrielle Wittner, and several others who contributed but did not want to be identified.

Special friends who have provided valuable input and unwavering support—Mary Kaye Fenwick, Martha Kipke, Linda Tillman, Julio Sasaki, Cheryl Thomas, Vic and Lorna Tirol.

My sister, Ella G. Bray, for her encouragement and absolute belief in my writing ability; daughter Michelle Ann Gekosky and friend Martha H. Kipke, for initially reviewing my drafts for logic and perspective.

My immediate family—Papa Doy Gallares; Mama Ekit (deceased); Mommy Gigi; brothers Angie, Nino, Judd, Larry (deceased); sisters Judette Gallares, Luchi Gallares-Stephens, Marj Kanaski, and Pam Gallares-Oppus.

My husband, Eddie, who continues to support my goals even though he knows writing books at night and weekends is not going to be easy, since I have a full-time, demanding job.

My mentor, Rob Jolles, who guided me from the first stages of putting together a proposal to submitting a manuscript. Even though I got impatient sometimes, you always told me during our telephone conversations to "hang in there"—I am grateful.

And to my publisher and lead editor, Bruce Fries, who gave me the opportunity to write this book.

Contents

List of Tables

Prologue

Chung Pak, a Korean American, was born in 1958 and came to America in 1971 with his family. He became a naturalized U.S. citizen in 1976 during a monumental occasion—the Bicentennial. Because of his limited English, he had to repeat sixth grade in a public school in Alabama. The small southern town where Chung and his family resided for a number of years had no special programs for immigrants. He was on his own to adjust to this new culture.

Why Alabama? Chung had an aunt who lived in the countryside, south of Montgomery. He learned to speak English on his own. This was especially difficult in the beginning, because his parents spoke little English. He learned by watching TV and by talking to American kids. One thing he excelled in was math. Math studies did not require excellent English skills.

After arriving in America, Chung's parents initially worked in a sweatshop and then a chicken-processing factory before being able to open their own restaurant. To finance the restaurant, they joined a *kye* (pronounced key), which is the pooling of money usually practiced by Koreans and Korean-Americans. Where Chung lived, people who joined the *kye* had to be trusted fully by the captain responsible for it. Sometimes it failed because some could not put their money into it every month or because others ran off after collecting their $10,000, so they would not have to repay their loans. The captain was responsible for these failures.

Chung was animated while he recounted his life story to me. Relating his experience as an American of Asian descent, he began his story here.

> I felt some discrimination. Certain people in America had preconceived notions about people who looked different and spoke with an accent. I have an accent in part because I grew up in Alabama. In Alabama, it was difficult to learn English correctly since certain letters, such as Ts, are often silent (like saying 'Alana' instead of Atlanta).
>
> The biggest barrier to not speaking English well is that we spoke Korean at home and my parents spoke only limited

English. Life went on and we tried our best to adjust to American life. It was not easy, but we had to learn the American culture in order to blend into the mainstream.

When I reached college age, I went to Auburn University and majored in chemical engineering. I pursued this major because I heard that as an engineer I would have greater job security and receive the highest salary.

After graduating, I got a job as a patent examiner at the United States Patent and Trademark Office and, after a short time, was promoted to primary patent examiner. While working during the day and supporting a wife and two children, I attended Catholic University Law School in Washington, DC, at night and earned a law degree.

Soon after graduating from law school, I accepted a job as a Union Carbide (later Praxair, Inc.) corporate counsel responsible for the company's intellectual property matters in Connecticut. I was considered one of Praxair's best and top corporate lawyers. I moved back to the Washington, DC area after I was appointed as an administrative patent judge at the Board of Patent Appeals and Interferences.

When asked, "As a minority, what do you think of the glass ceiling?" I replied, "It exists in both private and federal public sectors." Several factors contribute to it, one of which is having an accent. In my experience, people make prejudgments that you are not a good communicator, writer, or speaker if you have an accent.

When I became a patent examiner in 1982, there were not many Asian-American professionals. I had to work twice as hard as most examiners to climb the career ladder.

When I sought a major promotion to obtain greater responsibility and authority, I was denied. Although I received an "outstanding" rating in the initial evaluation stage, the supervisors deemed I was "less than satisfactory" in the final stages of the evaluation. The supervisors alleged that I made thirteen patent examining errors. The legal criteria used involved somewhat subjective judgment calls and were open to different interpretations. Because I felt strongly about protecting my professional reputation and credibility, I requested a reconsideration of this rating. To substantiate my positions, I wrote an over thirty-page brief setting forth my arguments and supplied over a hundred pages of documentation as supporting evidence. After a five-hour presentation, I was successful in persuading the supervisors and director to change the rating to "outstanding."

I won my first case as an attorney and I was my first client. This victory gave me great confidence. Even though I prevailed, that experience left a sour taste in my mouth because of the overwhelming obstacles that I had to overcome to obtain this promotion. That experience led to my decision to leave the federal government and join Union Carbide as its corporate counsel.

I always believed in my potential and knew that I would make it through perseverance in the face of adversity.

Being active in my community, with the goal of helping fellow immigrants, other ethnic groups, and even native-born Americans, I engage in multiple activities as part of my involvement in support groups. These activities help new immigrants to assimilate quickly into American society.

Many of the free services that my network of professionals and I offer to the community are education programs and seminars. The two- to three-year programs are well attended by ethnic groups that want to take advantage of free education or the "how-to" seminars. Discussions on cross-cultural or diversity topics help people adjust quickly to American society and ease them out of the initial culture shock that most experience during their first few years in America.

The major concern that ethnic groups have is who to turn to and what services can they get. My colleagues and I tackle many issues that range from citizen safety, immigration and legal issues to education and employment. In many cases, people ask questions on citizen safety issues, especially how to avoid becoming innocent victims of hate crime.

I fill in the gaps by asking help from police officers who, like myself, are actively involved with events in the Gaithersburg and Germantown, Maryland (suburbs of Washington, DC), communities. In the recent past, hate crimes were rampant in

> our communities. To alleviate people's fears, we discuss the many signs of hate crimes, why they happen, and which particular groups are obvious targets.
>
> The lawyers talk about immigration issues, domestic problems, and job discrimination. This is a service that many people welcome, especially the new arrivals, since they do not know where to start and who to go to for help. In addition to open discussions and question-and-answer sessions, I provide literature and brochures that give people resources in case they need help.

Chung's efforts are a testament to his commitment and dedication to helping others. He believes that if he shares his strategies, he is also helping others to lead meaningful personal and professional lives. His advice is to select the strategies that work best for you, use them again and again, and share them with others who might be able to benefit from them.

Instead of feeling sorry for himself, Chung worked harder and did not accept defeat. Overcoming each disappointment made him stronger and more confident. Life went on and he tried his best to adjust to American life and culture. It was not easy, but he learned to blend into the mainstream.

Coming to America, Chung says, is much like starting a new life. You have to embrace a new culture, lifestyle, and customs without "letting go" of old values, customs, beliefs, and traditions from your home country. You might struggle in the beginning, like many people who come to this country for the first time. The challenges you meet range from financial to emotional. Being far away from family and friends and not knowing when you will see them again is a lonely feeling. Overcoming obstacles that might impede your goals and dreams in the beginning is only one stage. Once you have settled in and have accepted that some problems will always be there and that many obstacles, such as stereotyping, are caused by ignorance more than intention, you will find that you can focus more on yourself and move forward.

Most of the people interviewed for this book came from developing countries, except for Bill Skea and Lina Shoobridge from the U.K., Gabrielle Wittner from Switzerland, and Georg Hirsch from

Germany. But they all had strong goals and pushed themselves to the limit because, as they said, they had nothing to lose and everything to gain. They came to America for the long term.

Starting a new life in America meant adjustments in many areas—culture, language, lifestyle, social integration, job and economic adaptation, to name a few. Although many people felt lonely, confused, or even lost in the beginning, friends, family and relatives made adjustments easier. Support systems and help from communities also paved the way for people new to America to feel welcomed and accepted into society. Newfound friends (fellow immigrants and native-born Americans) filled the emotional void as people to talk to and socialize with. Among the new arrivals, those most willing to accept the many differences benefited more as they integrated into society.

I am one of those who came from a developing country. When I first entered America in 1971, through Seattle, I was young, single, and naïve. Because I came unprepared, I was also insecure and anxious. I did not know what to expect from the Immigration and Naturalization Service (INS), nor did I know what they expected from me.

When my turn came to be interrogated by an immigration officer, it was difficult. As I handed my passport and round-trip ticket to the immigration officer, he asked, "What would a young woman like you be doing in New York City with a tourist visa?" I told the officer that I was going to visit relatives, but when he scrutinized my passport, it did not have the name and address of my relatives. I had left that section blank unintentionally because I did not think it was that important. That oversight of mine triggered some doubt. The officer told me to step aside, because he had more questions to ask but did not want the people behind me to be delayed.

I did not know what was happening, but in a matter of minutes, another immigration officer approached and invited me to go to a room to answer further questions from a panel of other officers. I was calm and intense, although deep within I was angry. The officers seemed frustrated because all my answers were appropriate and focused. I did not waver, because there was nothing more for me to say. During the lengthy interrogation, two immigration officers switched their strategy by speaking in Spanish to prevent me from understanding what they were going to do next. Before they could even ask me the questions, I had already opened my carry-on bag to show the contents. Both looked at me and said, "So you know Spanish too?"

At that point, they told me to go and that they would arrange for the next flight to take me from Seattle to New York City. Exhausted, I looked for a public phone so I could call my relatives and give them my new flight schedule.

First, I had to find a phone and figure out how to use it. I did not know how to make the call, how much money it would take, when to put the coins in, how to get "long distance." I could have called collect but decided I could use my own money without even checking if I had enough coins. I wandered around looking for a Traveler's Aid, but there was not one close by, so I went to a fast food restaurant and asked if they could exchange my money. They did and I asked how to use the phone. It was a minor but common obstacle, which would have been much harder if I did not speak English.

However, not everyone will go through this type of ordeal. Thousands of people come to America every day from all over the world. They go through the same process as everyone else. They fall in line, answer questions, get passports stamped, pass customs inspection, pick up their luggage, and are on their way.

Introduction

America is a nation of immigrants and is becoming increasingly multiethnic and multicultural: a melding of social and cultural differences of people from all over the world. I chose to write this book to relate the real-life experiences of immigrants and to satisfy personal reasons, because I, too, was one of them. Their issues and struggles, and now successes, were as close to their hearts as mine were to me.

The people I interviewed for this book came to America when they were young and single. Adventurous, curious, seeking a better life, and armed with a positive outlook and determination, they worked hard in the beginning so that they might later taste the fruits of their labor. Now, all are doing well professionally and economically. I am proud to have had the opportunity to speak with them and get to know them personally. Their reflections often brought back memories—happy and sad. I asked all of them, Why America? The overwhelming response was, "When you are in a faraway land and you see beautiful postcards and you hear that America is the land of opportunity; who could resist?"

I was fortunate to interview many individuals from many different countries and ethnic backgrounds. Most agreed that moving to another country was not easy. It required elaborate preparation, much expense, giving up personal relations at home, and often learning a new language and culture.

Everyone learned along the way. Even with earlier struggles and frustrations, they remained optimistic, with future dreams and aspirations very much in their minds and hearts. Their anecdotes were both interesting and inspirational. Everyone pursued his or her goals to the maximum.

No one said he or she failed. Instead, they said they learned many lessons. Those who struggled more than others, on arriving and during their earlier years living in America, felt no bitterness. Surviving, earning a living, and achieving a goal were topmost in their minds. No one dwelt on self-pity. All just kept moving forward.

About This Book

Succeeding in America teaches strategies for success, based on the experiences of people who came to this country from all over the world seeking a better future. Contributors to this book wanted to tell their stories as they happened so that readers can gain insight into what they had to overcome to achieve the American dream.

This book is structured to appeal to several types of readers, so some sections will naturally be more relevant than others to your needs and interests. You should simply skip over any sections that do not interest you or meet your needs.

Parts One and Two are focused on our primary audience—people who already are in America. Part Three is intended for those who plan to come to America in the future. The appendices provide lists of valuable resources, such as associations, government agencies, colleges and universities, diversity programs, useful books and Web sites.

Part I

Working and Living in the United States

1. Understanding Cultural Differences

Understanding a country's culture is important to help you adjust to the new environment quickly. You can learn the basics by reading books, but to fully understand a country's culture, you need to experience it firsthand. Before you can understand the differences between cultures, you have to know what culture is and how it works.

Craig Storti, author of *Figuring Foreigners Out*, defines culture as a group's shared assumptions, values, and beliefs, which result in characteristic behavior. Storti's definition captures two essential points about culture: the invisible dimension (assumptions, values, and beliefs) and the visible dimension (behavior). These two dimensions are related to each other like cause and effect.[1]

The people I interviewed had different perspectives and experiences when it came to adjusting to a new culture. Most looked back at their earlier years in America in a positive light—as learning experiences rather than as mistakes or failures—a natural part of living in a new country. First and foremost, they experienced culture shock because everything was new and different.

Culture Shock

What is culture shock? Culture shock is when you face or experience a culture much different from yours. When you come from a country that has a different set of behaviors and attitudes, adapting to life in America can be shocking at first. You can choose to accept it and adjust to the differences, or you can resist it and suffer the results. Most of the people I interviewed struggled initially, but ultimately adjusted.

Take the experience of Sam Quaye from Ghana.

Sam owns and drives his own cab to make a living for his family. Sam's original intent was to come to America to study, but his plan changed when he arrived. Instead, he ended up working as a truck driver until he was financially able to be his own boss. One problem arose when he married a naturalized U.S. citizen from Ghana. The shock he experienced was that he had come to America with certain expectations of acting superior to women, as he always had back in Ghana, where women are responsible for running the household. He was surprised that his wife asked him to help with housework.

Sam thought he could live the same kind of life he had back in Ghana. He said, "The first time I had to take the trash out, I was surprised and angry. I never took the trash out in Ghana, why should I do it here? I told my wife, a Ghanaian herself, that she should do it and that she should act like the women back home. Well, my words went into deaf ears. I could not get away from doing my share of the chores. My wife was already liberated, having adjusted to being an American and accepting the lifestyle in America. It did not dawn on me that I had to be an equal partner with a woman. It startled me at first, but I learned to share the housework before too long. It is not about liking it, but a matter of adjusting and accepting the way things are."

Others have experienced various episodes of culture shock that could be attributed to ignorance and lack of understanding of American culture.

When I was living in Washington, DC, soon after I came to the United States, I went to a grocery store to buy food. (Going to the grocery became my regular task since I did not know how to do anything else domestic.) I was eager to start. Once I reached the nearby grocer, I asked the butcher if he could give me a "kilo" of pork. The butcher asked, while looking at me, "Which country do you come from?" I quickly said, "Sorry, I am from the Philippines and I meant 2.2 pounds."

Another experience, which I vividly remember, was when a roommate asked me to call a number to find out the weather forecast for the next day. I did not do it because I did not know what to say. My roommate said, "You are silly. It is only a recording. All you do is listen." I did not know that. In my home country, a person—not a machine—answered the phone.

Another hilarious experience that a friend told me about is when she picked up a friend from the bus stop. As she was nearing the stop, she noticed that her friend was pacing around so she asked her why. Her friend pointed to the bus stop sign, which said, "No standing."

Not everyone who came to America experienced culture shock. Many, such as Lina Shoobridge, had an easier time adjusting. Lina came to America from the U.K. because her father was assigned to the British Embassy as part of his tour of duty. She did not see any significant differences between American and U.K. culture, since English is the native language of both countries and the lifestyles are more or less the same.

As the people I interviewed overcame their initial culture shock, they found out there was so much more to learn. Next was learning how to meet new friends, talk to neighbors, and socialize. The time to fully adjust varied from person to person. It was easier for those who were open-minded and flexible, and more difficult for others who were more set in their ways.

Remember that America stands for life, liberty, and the pursuit of happiness and that Americans can be very informal compared to people from other countries. In America, some children call their parents by their first names (although this is not a common practice) and telephone them at work. Many people call their bosses by their first names rather than "Mister" or "Sir" or "Mrs." or "Ma'am" as in many developing countries.

Assimilation

Assimilation is the process of responding, accepting, and conforming to a new culture. Many Americans, both those who favor and those who oppose assimilation, believe that for immigrants to assimilate they must abandon their original cultural attributes and conform entirely to the behaviors and customs of the majority of the native-born population. For instance, in the terminology of the armed forces, assimilation represents a model of "up or out"—either immigrants bring themselves "up" to native cultural standards, or they are doomed to live "out" of the charmed circle of the national culture.

Many contributors told me that to them assimilation meant sharing different perspectives. Not surprisingly, older people found it more difficult to adjust because of their deeply ingrained values, customs, traditions, and beliefs. Although they eventually adjusted to American culture, many still express some desire for the way things used to be in their own countries.

In contrast, younger immigrants easily adjusted to almost everything, as if they had lived in America all their lives. Children born to immigrant parents are Americans through and through. They think and act like Americans. Although parents continue to tell their children about old customs, values, traditions, and beliefs, they are not sure if their children really listen. If their children pay attention, do they understand or care? Some shrug off their parents' stories with comments such as, "That was *your* life, Mom or Dad, not ours."

In the book *We Are All Multiculturalists Now,* Nathan Glazer writes, "Assimilation is not today a popular term. … Indeed, in recent years it has been taken for granted that assimilation—as an expectation of how different ethnic and racial groups would respond to their common presence in one society—is rejected. Had I asked what they thought of the term 'Americanization,' the reaction would have been more hostile."[2]

When you are experiencing culture shock, the easiest way to deal with it is to accept, or at least learn to live with, the differences. If you choose to accept or tolerate the differences, you can adapt quickly to a new country. But if you refuse to accept the differences, you will ultimately suffer the results and it will take longer for you to integrate into society. Isolating yourself defeats the purpose of social integration.

Relationships

Building new relationships is often easier on the job or at social functions, because interacting with others is more natural. When you are new on the job, your boss usually introduces you to people you will be working with. In social functions, a friend may introduce you to others. Interaction with others is essential, whether you are in America or elsewhere, because it allows you to meet new friends and develop support systems.

As they adjusted to American culture, most immigrants I interviewed began to interact first with fellow immigrants, whether from their own or other countries. Nilofer Qureshi, a Pakistani who joined her husband in America, said, "You make friends based on likes and dislikes and viewpoints. Ethnicity should not be a factor."

As new arrivals continued to grow culturally, they also expanded their relationships to include people outside of their cultures. They began to understand what it meant to be an American and how American culture was different from other cultures (voting and honoring American traditions and holidays, for example). They also began to decide what to retain from their own cultures, such as values and pride in their heritage.

Making friends

Sam Quaye discovered new friends from other former British colonies. Sam said, "I was lucky to build a social life with people I was comfortable with and could exchange pleasantries and share stories and personal lives." He made new friends at work and from socializing with people from his own country, who, in turn, introduced him to others.

However, many people are shy and find it difficult to introduce themselves to others. While it is easy for some who are naturally friendly and outgoing, not everyone is good at approaching strangers and engaging in small talk.

Nora Szeto, who is originally from Hong Kong, finds it difficult to approach people and introduce herself. Nora's solution to meeting people is through church activities, where she is friendly with a mix of people from different countries, including the United States.

Like Nora, I was also quite shy but I overcame this shyness early on, knowing that if I kept to myself I would be lonely and alone. And knowing that I was on my own, I realized that I had to either reach out or be left out, so I made a conscious decision to do my best to reach out. At first, assimilating into American society and interacting with new people made me anxious. It took courage and advice from friends to work it out. What helped most of all was when people approached me first, because approaching strangers was a struggle I had to overcome slowly. In time, I overcame my shyness by learning how to approach people and introduce myself, engaging in small talk, and using humor to relax. As I continued to spend more time with people, I became more comfortable and confident.

On top of all other cultural issues, people coming from non-English-speaking countries often find it difficult to integrate into American society because of language. Take gestures, for instance. In Bulgaria, or in India, to signal "yes" you shake your head from side to side, which is the opposite of the practice in the United States.

Interaction with coworkers

Getting along with coworkers is critical if you plan to stay employed. If you shy away from coworkers, they will hesitate to approach you. Involvement with others in a positive, compassionate way is crucial to success at work.

Sam Quaye, a former Ghanaian and now a naturalized U.S. citizen, worked as a truck driver until he could save enough money to buy and drive his own cab. From the beginning, Sam got along well with his fellow coworkers and often engaged in meaningful conversations with them. But as with many people, Sam also has close friends with whom he is more comfortable socializing. Since Sam socialized mostly with fellow Ghanaians, they shared the same culture, and getting along well was easy. When it came to socializing with others from different cultures, Sam treated them with respect just as he would any other person. Sam also believed that if he were in their shoes, these newfound friends would treat him the same way.

Julio Sasaki, a Peruvian, came to America to complete his post-graduate studies in industrial psychology. Like Sam, Julio also found a handful of people whom he considered friends in the strict sense of the word. Julio reached out to new coworkers by asking them to lunch or chatting with them during coffee breaks. By learning more about them, he found out that they could work well together—he helped them learn how to interpret data and they helped him create statistical tables. For Julio, sharing knowledge became a positive link to others.

Following are examples of activities that will help you get along smoothly with coworkers or others in your workplace:

- Ask a mentor (informal advisor) to give general guidance.
- Ask your manager to assign a buddy who can help you during your first few months on the job.
- Take someone to lunch to get to know him or her better.
- Ask a coworker for advice on a new project.
- Offer to help a coworker on a complex project.

Dating

Dating practices in America can be very different from other countries. In America, adults generally are freer than in most other countries. They can come and go as they please, with no curfews, no parents to dictate what they can or cannot do, or whom they should or should not go out with. It is a far cry from native homelands where parents still cling to old values, even when children are adults. When adults continue to live with their parents, they are often expected to follow the old rules.

In Elena Minnitti's case, she expected a monogamous relationship. She said, "My boyfriend was American. I found out that in America, guys often see other girls, too, even if they are already in a relationship. It was not entirely a monogamous relationship as I saw it, so I broke up with my boyfriend because I did not want to give up my values, nor did I want to compromise. I always thought that I would find one good man for me who would stay with me forever. It happened eventually. I am now married to an Italian-American whom I met while in New York City."

If you come from an Eastern society, you may be shocked by a public show of affection such as kissing or touching, because, in your own country, these practices take place only behind closed doors. In public, for example, often people from certain cultures kiss the cheeks rather than the lips to show affection.

A person, who did not want to be identified, told me that in China, they follow a different practice when it comes to dating. No kissing. Few intimacies. No sex before marriage. "Because men could not touch us," she explained, "they tended to be romantic in other ways, such as taking us to see a movie, and bringing us flowers and chocolates. When I moved to America, dating was more shocking.

I am not sure if the intimacy the people showed when dating was real or simply common practice. I thought if women do not allow men to touch them, then the relationship would not go any further."

It is risky for foreigners to date Americans at all unless they understand what is an appropriate location, how much touching is allowed, and who is expected to pay the tab. The consensus from people I interviewed is that you should follow dating practices that are comfortable to you. You should not merely follow the dictates of American dating practices, but be sure that what you do is what you truly believe in your heart.

Some examples of dating practices that you might find comfortable would be to pair with another couple during the early stages of dating or to first go on a lunch date to get acquainted in a more relaxed way. When you go out with someone you could explore those things you have in common—watching a sporting event, for example—in order to give your friendship a boost in the right direction. In deciding where to go, it helps considerably to discuss it first with the other person. Select a place that you both enjoy, such as a museum or a movie, and preferably choose a movie that you *both* want to see.

Shopping

Shopping in America is often different compared to other countries. In many developing countries, especially in small towns and villages, shopping is special and reserved for certain days, like Friday. On these days, townsfolk usually buy meat products, which are not everyday meals, while people in America do not have the same obstacle. They can buy meat products anytime, anywhere.

When it comes to buying nonfood items, haggling (bargaining) is still a practice that continues in many places outside the United States, especially in open markets and small stores in the outskirts of major cities. The practice continues because it is fun. You cannot tell who is fooling whom. Dave Lang said that in Vietnam, haggling is common everywhere. Although the prices of many items are theoretically fixed, buyers resort to bargaining anyway, because it is an accepted way of doing business.

In America, prices are generally fixed; yet haggling is quite common for some products like cars, and prices often vary from store to store. Warehouse stores generally have lower prices because you are buying in bulk, but boutiques and specialty retail stores usually have higher prices.

Although haggling is less common in America, many stores are perpetually in a sale mode, and people tend to take advantage of lower prices. If you are planning to buy something, such as an appliance, it is wise to wait until the item goes on sale. You can save money this way, especially if you do not need the appliance or item right away. Or you can buy items when they are on sale and keep them until needed. If you make "impulse purchases," you may feel bad when these same products go on sale later at much lower prices.

Shopping in the United States can be done in several ways: You can drive to stores, order from a catalog, or shop through the Internet. With the Internet, you can browse the product catalog electronically and pay for the items by credit card. Shopping online is a nice option if you are too busy to go out and shop.

Sales tax

Many newcomers to America are either confused or surprised by sales taxes. Sales taxes vary depending on the state where you shop. For example, if you shop in Virginia, the sales tax is 4.5 percent, while in Maryland it is 5 percent. And even more interesting is when you shop in states that only charge sales tax for luxury items. For example, I visited an outlet store in West Virginia and I was charged sales tax for buying an umbrella, which the store lists as a luxury item. I told the store clerk, "You must be kidding." The store clerk responded with an emphatic "No. I only work here and I am following store policies."

For Georg Hirsch, from Germany, shopping "was a bit of a culture shock." The most obvious example is the tax added to most goods. More subtle but equally important is the fact that some goods don't do you much good unless you buy something else that is needed to make it work, such as computer software that only works if you buy a new piece of hardware, or vice versa. In many cases, these additional needs are not mentioned when something is advertised.

"And not everything is a bargain," Georg emphasized. "You should also think about air fares that seem very cheap, but they might be low-cost one-way fares, based on a round-trip purchase. Another field where you need to be on top of your toes is e-commerce. For example, a computer company advertises that its latest version of particular software only costs $29.99, plus tax and shipment. As you go through the menus to purchase it, they recommend that you buy a warranty and one-year upgrade plan, plus two other pieces of software (the decision by default is always 'Yes, add it to my shopping cart'). The company tells you initially that you would get something outstanding for less than $30, but unless you actively fend off all the extras, you end up with a total of $130."

Tips for shopping in America

Remember, except for certain purchases, such as new cars and yard sales, there is little or no haggling over prices. Before you buy something, read the available information carefully. There are a number of useful sources, such as *Consumer Reports* magazine, where you can obtain information about various products. You can contact the local Better Business Bureau to inquire if there have been any problems reported with a particular business. Be on the lookout for sales. Remember to think about whether you really need an item right away. If you do not have an immediate need, wait for the item to go on sale or take time to shop around—often you can find the same item at a much lower price.

As well as being alert for sales, you should also be wary of sales. Keep in mind that just because something is advertised as being on sale, that doesn't mean that the price is a good one. Be aware of the possibility of extra charges, such as shipping charges associated with online shopping and catalogs. Make sure when you buy something that your purchase is complete and that you don't need something else to go with it. For example, you may buy an electric toy, and then find out that you have to pay separately for necessary batteries.

With advancing technology, you can now shop electronically for almost anything. It used to be that you would order from a catalog, mail your order, and wait for items to be delivered. Now you can order online, since more and more companies sell their products and services through the Internet. Shopping electronically has become especially convenient for busy people. And since many households have computers, it is easy to log on at night when the children are asleep or when you have free time. You can go from one Web site to another to compare prices.

Dress/Fashion

People wear clothes that fit their lifestyles and personalities. Some wear fancy clothes because they meet current trends while others wear what they can afford, and still others wear whatever clothes they want whether they look good in them or not.

Many older people from other countries who live in America still wear native clothes, such as the *barong* (Philippines), the *sari* (India), or the *guyabera* (Cuba). However, these native clothes are often worn only during special holidays and certain social events. For example, many people wear the *barong* on Philippine Independence Day, which is celebrated by Filipinos in America.

According to Georg Hirsch, "Germans tend to emulate Americans. When I went to school in Iowa in the late 1980s, it took me a while to get over baseball caps worn the other way around. A few years later, I saw a member of the national soccer team of Germany sporting a baseball cap, and guess which way he wore it!"

"Oh yes, as I think about it," Georg said, "There *are* some differences between the United States and Germany. The first American bank I ever visited was in Iowa, and the month was August. I was baffled when I saw customers wearing shorts and beach sandals, while addressing bank clerks by their first names. Unthinkable scenario in Germany!"

You can dress in your own native costumes even when you are in America. America is a nation built entirely of different groups of people, and it is well understood that some dressing practices are dictated by religious beliefs, like those of Muslims.

Many American men view women who dress seductively or behave flirtatiously as sending a message that they want to be approached. Even if wearing short skirts or low-cut dresses most of the time is customary in your home country, it may not be appropriate for many situations in America.

Some organizations, especially in the public sector (military, fire and rescue, police, etc.), mandate wearing a uniform. In a way, this practice is beneficial since it avoids competition for status. Everyone is dressed the same way every day. As an added bonus, it also avoids extra expense, especially important where salaries are meager. In the private sector, you can normally wear what you want; however, many companies have dress codes that limit your choices.

In America, school children do not customarily wear uniforms except in some private schools. But in other countries, especially in Asia, most schools require that students wear uniforms to school. This is true for both public and private schools. Just as it can be advantageous wearing a uniform in some government jobs, in many ways uniforms offer an advantage to parents who do not have much spending money or do not want to be concerned that their children are under pressure to buy designer clothes in order to compete with other students.

Whichever country you come from, be considerate and dress appropriately. Doing so is respectful of the country you live in. If you are used to a certain way of dressing in your homeland, you can continue to do so based on what you are comfortable with. But do not ignore the fact that if you attend a formal dinner, for instance, you are expected to dress accordingly. It is important to remember that there is a place for everything.

Just because something is “fashionable,” that does not mean it will look good on you. On the other hand, something might look good on you even if it is not “fashionable.” And if it is pleasing, you just might start a fashion trend.

Tips for deciding what to wear

To find out what is appropriate dress, observe the people around you. Native costumes may be worn in some instances, if you are comfortable in them, or if required by your religion. In America, people tend to break fashion rules. So just because you see something, that does not mean it is in fashion.

2. Getting the Right Education

In the United States, your educational background counts heavily toward the chances of getting a job in your chosen career. Employers are looking for specialists, people with the education and skills who can go right into a position with a minimum of training. The right type of college degree can help open the door to a job that meets your interests.

Many of the people interviewed for this book could not afford to take leaves of absence from work to go back to school. Instead, most worked full-time and went to school at night. They felt that the effort was worth it, because without a proper education they simply could not compete with the many qualified people employers have to choose from.

Obtaining an Education

It's important to get a good education if you want to make it in America professionally and economically. Although education is only one determining factor, it plays a major role in getting a good job and advancing in your chosen career. Good jobs are available, but the criteria for getting them have changed significantly, with more and more people going back to school to pursue advanced studies and compete for well-paying jobs.

For example, Maria Jaramillo from Mexico, a former elementary schoolteacher who is now retired, started taking classes at Pima College, an extension school in Nogales, Arizona. She completed her associate's degree in Liberal Arts at Imperial Valley College in El Centro, California, but continued to take classes at another extension school in Calexico, located at the border of Mexico and the United States. Maria took advanced classes in education so that she could get the opportunity to teach high school classes. Maria's additional credentials helped her to get a better job at a much higher salary.

Julio Sasaki is of Japanese descent, but was born and raised in Peru. He completed his doctoral degree in industrial psychology from Bowling Green University in Ohio. Very independent by nature, Julio focused solely on his studies and did not socialize much.

After completing his doctoral degree, Julio worked at several jobs and is now a manager of management information systems (MIS). Julio said that obstacles turned into benefits and he now tastes the fruits of his labor knowing he earned them the hard way.

Although it takes perseverance, it also helps to remember sometimes that time spent socializing is time that could be spent studying or applying oneself more diligently. In studies, this is even truer while seeking a "doctorate" or writing a doctoral dissertation in a language that is not your native one.

Continuing your education from abroad

Getting a good education in America could be a lengthy process for those who come from abroad. You must be well organized to ensure that your application form and supporting documents are completed accurately. Typically, your first stop is to visit the embassy or consulate and learn what the requirements are to obtain a visa after gaining acceptance from a school. The consular office at the U.S. embassy in your home country is the place where you get the most help, but since you may not be the only applicant, you might have to wait a while to be interviewed. An exception might be if there is a specific date that you have to be in America to start your schooling. If so, be sure to mention this.

Evelyn Shu is from Hong Kong. She completed her undergraduate studies at UCLA in Los Angeles with a bachelor's degree in communication. Since she could not go directly to a university from a high school abroad, she had to first register in a junior college. She then transferred to UCLA from Pasadena City College after completing two years there. Although her parents paid for her tuition the first two years, she was able to get a scholarship from UCLA for her junior year. Evelyn benefited from completing her education in America. Her bachelor's degree helped her achieve a professional career in instructional design and development.

Bharat and Ravi Sahay are brothers who came from India separately in the 1970s. Both completed postgraduate degrees in engineering and succeeded in finding good jobs in big corporations that needed their highly specialized skills. Education paid off handsomely for both, although Ravi took a different route years later when he completed an MBA and ventured into an independent consulting business. Bharat decided to stay in the corporate world doing what he loves best—computer systems design.

Bharat and Ravi did not have the same worries financially as others did. Their transition from study to work was smooth primarily because they had visas that allowed them to work. By being able to work first, both brothers were able to enhance their skills in their chosen fields. They were also able to transfer practical work experience to their schoolwork.

I, too, took advanced studies in America, but only after sixteen years of living in the United States. I chose George Washington University because of its proximity to the World Bank. The only way I could pursue a job that interested me was to take graduate studies at an American school.

Applying for admission and scholarships

Scholarships are benefits given to students who excel academically. However, not everyone can get a scholarship to attend school in America. To be considered, you must achieve the criteria required by the school. These might include a minimum grade point average (GPA) and the ability to understand and speak English well. If you have difficulty in speaking or learning English, there are schools that provide special arrangements to accommodate your needs.

Before you gain acceptance to most graduate schools in America, you need to have an official transcript sent directly to your school. That should be easy enough, except that in foreign countries, processing often takes a long time. Getting grades translated to American equivalencies can be another obstacle. This is necessary so American schools can determine whether your GPA meets the entrance requirements for graduate studies.

Applying from abroad for a scholarship to study in America can be tedious. To help increase your chances of getting a scholarship, you may want to apply at several schools in your field of study.

Applying for a scholarship while you are already in America is easier. You have the advantage of proximity, time, and easy Internet access to required forms. And the best part is you can apply for different types of scholarships, which could include grants or financial aid.

Getting sponsorship by a large company that values your enhanced education and skills is a rare opportunity. Such opportunities are more evident in the science fields, because employees with specialized skills (chemistry, for instance) are not easy to come by. For example, Elena Minnitti was granted a scholarship to complete her doctoral degree in chemistry at New York University and was offered a research scientist position upon graduation. Elena was fortunate to get a job she desired because of her specialized skills, advanced degree, and previous job experience.

Grade equivalency

Grades are measured differently in many countries. Table 1 includes grade equivalency estimates for several countries.

Table 1 - Grade Equivalency

America	India	Hong Kong	Peru	Philippines
A (4.0 GPA)	First Class (Honors / Distinction) 75% & above	A	17-20	90 & above
B (3.0 GPA)	First Class (60% & above)	B	15-17	80-90
C (2.0 GPA)	Second Class (45% & above)	C	13-15	75-79
D (1.0 GPA)	Third Class (30% & above)	D	11-13	Not applicable
F	Fail (Below 30%)	F	10 or less	Below 75

Types of Schools

Throughout the United States, you can find private and public schools—colleges and universities, community colleges and vocational schools. You may choose to go to a community college for a two-year degree because the tuition is more affordable; or if money is available, you may choose a four-year college. If you are interested in vocational schools, you can also look for information in libraries, telephone directories, and via the Internet. You may also be able to obtain help from friends and your community, depending on the specialty you want to pursue. Once you have the information, call and arrange to talk to an advisor or the Director of Admissions. If the school is in your area, visit the location to see if it meets your needs.

Colleges and Universities

If you plan to further your studies, you can find colleges and universities in every major city. If money is a problem, you can apply for a student loan or tuition aid at the school you plan to attend. It is wise to get as much information as you can about the kind of degree you want and what is offered by each of the schools you are interested in. If you are not in the immediate area, you can call the registrar's office of the school and request that a prospectus or brochure be mailed to you. If the school you are interested in is in your area, you might find it useful to make an appointment to talk to an advisor so you can have your questions answered before you make a decision on enrolling.

Each school can provide prospective students with information about itself and the degrees it offers. For example, the following schools are academically strong in certain disciplines: Carnegie Mellon University in Pennsylvania—engineering and industrial management, Rice University in Texas—architecture, Amherst College in Massachusetts—psychology, Duke University in North Carolina—history and chemistry, Massachusetts Institute of Technology—economics, and Northwestern University in Illinois—journalism.[3]

Community colleges

Classes in community colleges are generally more affordable and easier to gain admission to. The tuition might be within your reach even if you do not have enough money to enroll in a four-year college or university. Since community colleges offer only two-year educational programs, you will have to transfer those credits to a four-year college or university and finish another two years to complete your undergraduate degree.

If you have a particular university in mind to transfer to after obtaining a two-year degree, or perhaps even earlier, it is extremely important that you make sure the classes you are taking at the community college level will earn credit when you transfer. Some students take classes at a "junior college" or two-year community campus only to discover, with great disappointment, that few if any of these classes are recognized when they transfer. This is an issue that can get very complicated, since a university might say that it accepts a particular course for credit but still may acknowledge credit for only a limited number of community college courses in a particular field—or as they apply to a specific degree.

The good news is there is plenty of help available, and there are counseling offices in many junior colleges to help advise students on which courses might be acceptable for credit at various universities. You also can obtain information by contacting the university. They will probably be happy to know that you hope to enroll there, and often will go out of their way to assist you.

Vocational schools

Vocational schools are another option for those who are good with their hands or who want to specialize in a trade. You can obtain information on vocational schools from libraries, local telephone yellow pages, the Internet, or your friends and community. Once you have the information, call and arrange to talk to an advisor or director of admissions. If the school is in your area, visit the location to see if the particular school meets your needs and interests.

You can find a variety of vocational schools, depending on the field of study you want to focus on. Examples of jobs that you might find relevant courses for are: aviation maintenance technician, air traffic controller, automotive mechanic, and food service manager.

Distance learning

Distance learning is provided by many educational institutions via correspondence courses conducted by mail or the Internet. Virtual universities allow you to register online, read your assignments electronically, and receive self-paced materials. Many universities use a method called computer-based training. These types of schools either send you a CD-ROM or allow you to take classes online after you have registered, received instructions, and selected your password. This way you are in control of your time.

For example, when I registered for a course in "Effective Written Communication" a few years ago, I chose the self-paced workbooks. I talked to the evaluator assigned to me by phone when I had questions about homework assignments. I was not on my own. This was like being in school, but for me it was better because I worked at my own pace and was able to concentrate on doing my homework in the peace and quiet of my own home. It was a challenge to do this at night in addition to other work I was responsible for. With this approach, immigrants avoid being embarrassed in the classroom environment where they have to speak in front of others, and where, if their knowledge of English is limited, they may avoid speaking out and submit their homework without participating in discussions.

Mindedge (*www.mindedge.com*) is an example of a Web resource for adult learning, training, and continuing education. Another source of learning through the Internet is the Computer Institute (*www.trainus.com*), which provides free technology seminars. If you are still in high school and love learning electronically, you can register at CyberSchool, a consortium of public school institutions throughout the United States that offers interactive distance learning. CyberSchool delivers high-quality courses via CD-ROMs, videotapes, workbooks, and Web sites such as *www.cyberschool.k12.or.us.*

Special schools

Adults and children who have learning disabilities, such as dyslexia, or behavioral and psychological problems, such as attention deficit disorder or autism, can find special schools to help them adapt to society, even if their social skills are limited. At these schools, help is available from tutors and highly trained teachers. You can find a list of these schools in your local telephone yellow pages, in relevant directories at the library, or you can search for them on the Internet.

Learning and Understanding English

Learning how to speak and write in English decently or even with sophistication is important when you want to get a good education. Despite some exceptions, English is the language of instruction in America. Your success in getting a good job after completing your studies could be determined by how well you did in school. It is important to learn English well before moving on to your next endeavor, because opportunities may be elusive if you cannot communicate your ideas clearly. Some things are easier said than done. You may not learn English as quickly as you intend and this may delay accomplishing your plans. It takes patience and effort, but in time, most immigrants significantly improve their language skills.

Learning and understanding English can be a major challenge if you come to America with little or no English. You have to start with the basics before you can speak English well. It could take years to learn how to speak English fluently, especially if you never spoke English in your home country. If you were exposed to English or used English in school, it is a matter of refining how you speak by using the right words, tenses, and proper pronunciation.

Some of the people I interviewed learned English formally by finding a tutor to provide individual instruction. They also learned informally by watching TV, listening to people speak, and reading newspapers. Others improved their English by watching movies with subtitles. (But watch out for those subtitles. They are not always accurate, and some of them are ridiculous!) Some of the people who came to America with very limited English took classes in English for speakers of other languages (ESOL).

Other people I interviewed already knew English but could not speak the language fluently. Many were comfortable speaking English, although with an ethnic accent. Lina Shoobridge and Bill Skea from the U.K. were fortunate to have English as their native language.

Ellen Dimaano Latham originally emigrated to Canada from the Philippines and moved to America a few years later. She vividly remembers an anecdote that she still finds embarrassing. "The family I came to live with had just moved to a new house," Ellen explained. "Of course, with people like me who are used to hardwood floors, seeing carpeted floors was something new. The family told me that they have wall-to-wall carpeting. I gushed and the first thing I did was walk to the end of the room to feel the walls, and then I said, 'I don't feel the carpets on these walls.' I took the meaning literally." Embarrassment is something that comes to everyone. The thing to remember is that what might be a little embarrassing today will be good for sharing a laugh when you look at it in retrospect.

Following are a few examples of the consequences of mistranslations of common words:

- A painting contractor suggested that an employee wear shorts during hot weather so he would be more comfortable. The next day, the employee showed up for work in his underwear.
- In another instance, a hospital administrator told a temporary employee that hospital workers must not wear open-toed shoes. The next day, the employee wore sandals to work instead of shoes.

Julio Sasaki speaks Spanish as his native language and went to a British school to learn English. "I learned to speak and understand English, but it was not enough when I arrived in America to study," he said. "I had to meet several requirements to be accepted for a doctoral program at Bowling Green University in Ohio, including an English comprehension test."

Gabrielle Wittner is from Switzerland and speaks German as her native language. She came to America through a special agency as an au pair. Before coming to America, she went to Australia for three months to study English. She supplemented her learning by talking to people, watching TV and movies, and asking native English speakers exactly how things are said in English. But, being realistic, she added, "I still needed more training. When I first came to America, living with an American family helped me speak English better because I was taking care of a household of four: mom and three school-aged children and had to communicate with all of them."

Louis Cheng, from Taiwan, studied English in the United States and went to school at American University in Washington, DC, but as the owner of two restaurants, he needed to communicate even better. To improve his communication skills he talked to customers who frequented his restaurants. In the beginning of our interview, he said, "A restaurant business is a people business. You come across different types of people every day. You welcome them, create a relationship of friendship to encourage customers to come back and eat at your restaurants again, exchange pleasantries, and talk about new items on the menu." As Louis' English language skills improved, so did his business.

Georg Hirsch came from Germany to work as a foreign correspondent. In Georg's case, the difficulty mostly involved speaking with an accent. "When I was halfway through my master's degree in Iowa," he said, "I spent the summer break traveling 10,000 miles by car through the eastern part of the United States. To my surprise, I could understand the people down South rather well, but not vice versa! At a gas station in rural Tennessee, it was almost impossible to communicate to the clerk what I wanted. Having seen my license plate, he sincerely apologized for not understanding me, pointing out that he was not used to an Iowan accent. Today, I sometimes claim to be from Iowa when someone asks me first thing where I'm from."

Everyone I interviewed told me that speaking English is critical if you want to integrate into American society and ultimately succeed. Its importance must not be taken lightly. If people cannot communicate or relate to others, how do they expect others to understand them? Work with them? Socialize with them? For some who came to America with no knowledge of English, the language barrier was often frustrating and overwhelming.

Other people who struggled with the English language persevered and were eventually able to break the barrier. They learned how to speak English well by watching TV, listening to the radio, reading the newspaper, and by listening and observing how other people use English.

Speaking English as a professional

In general, if you are a highly specialized professional but speak only limited English, you are at a big disadvantage. Doctors and lawyers are specifically required to pass board and bar exams before being allowed to practice medicine and law in America. Even if you are armed with noteworthy credentials and extensive experience in your field, the drawbacks are obvious. You might be able to work in the medical field, but in a much lower-level job, such as a medical assistant or medical technologist, rather than a doctor, or in the legal field as a law clerk or paralegal, rather than a lawyer.

Such setbacks will surely affect your sense of dignity and self-respect. If you decide to stay in America despite the setbacks, you may have to swallow your pride and work in a lower-level job until you improve your English and establish the credentials required to practice your profession in America.

Writing in English

Writing well in English is an art. It does not come naturally for many people, even those who have English as their native language. Non-native English speakers tend to think in their own language when they write, translating individual words and sentences into English. It is dangerous to translate word for word because a word in another language may mean something different in English. So, when someone else reads what a non-native English speaker writes, the writing may not make sense because everything may be mixed up.

Several people admitted that for them, writing is a lot easier than speaking English, because writing lets them practice visually—how words and phrases are connected into sentences and paragraphs. Interestingly, when we talk we often use the first word that comes to mind. In writing, we get a second chance to replace that word with a better word, one that may more accurately convey what we want to say. But, in writing, not all of us take advantage of that second chance and still use the first word that comes to mind.

Ravi Sahay told me that in the beginning he learned to write, but in a convoluted, long-winded way. He said that when he started to learn how to write in English, one could get lost trying to read what he had written. "Garbled" was the word he used to describe his writing. Ravi said that when you learn a way of writing in your own country and you come to America, you have to basically unlearn what you previously knew.

It takes practice to sharpen your skills and write well. The more you write, the easier it becomes. Table 2 provides tips for writing well. For more information, read *Writing with Precision: How to Write So That You Cannot Possibly Be Misunderstood,* by Jefferson D. Bates. This handbook includes an extensive glossary of American idioms, developed to assist readers from other backgrounds and cultures. It also includes tips on usage of compound words, hyphenation, numeration, and capitalization.

Table 2 - Writing Tips

Do	Don't
Pay attention to detail	Be unprepared and neglect research
Organize your material to present a clear message (e.g., be neat, spellcheck, use correct grammar, use correct punctuation)	Be too messy or too rigid
Be precise by using words with exact meaning	Try to impress the reader with big, complex words
Have others review your manuscript drafts	Worry about getting it perfect on the first try
Be brief; avoid unnecessary words	Be wordy or redundant
Use short sentences	Use long sentences
Revise and edit multiple times	Be intimidated by having to revise

Resources for improving your English

Understanding English is much more than just learning English as a second language. It is also important to learn as much as possible about American history, culture, and traditions; and, of course, it is important to know the vocabulary in your area of expertise. There are many resources for improving your English.

When you are in America, you can learn English much more quickly than in your own country because everyone has to speak English. You can watch TV, talk to and socialize with English-speaking people, and take English classes. Classes in English as a second language are offered in many places in each city, and many people can also benefit from services such as adult education programs in public schools. In addition to standard classes, tutors are also available for those who want individual assistance. Schools that have predominantly high immigrant populations offer access to tutors. Having tutors available helps parents, as well as children who may need assistance with their homework.

It is worth emphasizing that learning and understanding English is a major advantage since English is the language used in all schools. If you are planning to seek a graduate or doctoral degree, it might be particularly difficult to gain acceptance if your English is limited. You should realize that advanced studies entail many open discussions, plus writing. If you know before you leave your home country that your verbal and written communication skills are weak, it would be wise to sharpen your skills before leaving.

It's also good to read English books as often as possible. Reading is vital if you want to learn English and to learn about the world. If English is your second language, listen to tape-recorded books while you follow along with a hard copy of the book. This will help your reading skills as well as your knowledge base.

3. Finding the Best Jobs

Finding a job that closely matches your qualifications and interests is not easy. This is where your patience is tested. It's not unusual for a job search to take anywhere from six weeks to two years. Many jobs are advertised in newspaper help-wanted classified ads and employment Web sites, but often people find that networking and personal recommendations are the best strategies for finding jobs in a competitive market.

Some of the people I interviewed had difficulties finding jobs at first, despite their qualifications. Many have bachelor's degrees in several fields, but work as support staff only because they graduated from foreign schools, and the companies they work for do not consider foreign schools to be at the same level as American schools.

The people who came to America with degrees in specialized fields found work quickly. Several are employed at companies that were looking for highly specialized workers in the science and technology fields and sponsored students who completed their degrees in America. Two factors helped these people find jobs more quickly: high-demand fields of study and graduation from American schools.

From my own experience, I know that many American employers assume that the university-level schools in other countries are not up to American standards, which is not necessarily true. Many foreign schools are every bit as good, or better than, their American counterparts.

Julio Sasaki found employment through help from classmates. Even with a doctors degree, he did not hesitate to start from the bottom just to earn money while supporting himself through college. He worked as a waiter in a restaurant close to school during his free days. After he graduated, he found his first job at a retail store as an analyst. Although it was not his ideal job, Julio needed professional work experience in quantitative (statistical) work.

Types of Jobs

You will find a wide variety of jobs in America in many different fields. Most of the people I interviewed are now working in jobs that interest them and match their qualifications.

Professional jobs

Professional jobs cover a range of expertise from individual contributors (e.g., generalists or specialists in different fields) to managers and executives. In most cases, the term "professional" is linked to people who are in exempt positions (salaried but not paid overtime). *Career Magazine* (a free publication) cites tens of thousands of professional job openings in all fields.

Information technology

A few of the people I interviewed found employment in the fields of information technology, computer systems design, and computer programming—jobs that are available in all parts of America. Technological start-up companies are sprouting not only in Silicon Valley, but also in Texas, Massachusetts, northern California, and in northern Virginia, an area with one of the largest concentrations of Internet employers in the country.

One person told me, "We are in such demand, especially when the Y2K issues came up. Major companies ran after us but since we had so many choices, money and benefits are what we went for. It is so competitive out there that we can take our time and wait for the best offer."

If you set your sights on careers in technology, you may also need to go back to school and update your skills. Perhaps you can work during the day and study at night. Many community colleges and universities offer degree programs in computer sciences. You can take advantage of any of these opportunities based on your needs and financial situation. If you work in a big company, you can often take advantage of tuition aid programs.

According to the *H-1B Visa Quota News*[4] the need for high-tech professionals is increasing. Many human resource managers from companies nationwide are seeking foreigners with prized technical skills, such as computer programmers and electrical engineers. H-1B visas are given to foreigners with college degrees to allow them to work in the United States for up to six years.

Education

Education as a career has become important due to the shortage of specialized teachers in America. The INS gave permission to the U.S. Department of Education to recruit people from other countries to teach many subjects, especially math. This is not to say anyone can qualify—the teachers are properly screened to ensure they have the proper credentials.

In the article "In Short Supply, Teachers Join Special Visa List,"[5] Gerry Chico, president of the Chicago Board of Education, said, "The way was paved for the recruitment of foreign teachers when the Labor Department certified the existence of a critical shortage of educators with certain specialties and agreed to approve candidates for special work certificates." Chico further said, "It's a hugely important program for public school education." He added, "We must find more teachers in our critical areas. If they are not available in the United States, we need to reach out to other countries."

Medical

If you are in the medical field, you should have a relatively easy time finding a job because, in the past few years, due to a shortage of critical personnel, hospitals have recruited doctors and nurses from other countries. Many countries use overseas recruitment centers to help process the paperwork. Doctors and nurses jump at these opportunities as a sure legal way to enter America. They usually come under H-1B visas, which are available only to workers in occupations requiring highly specialized knowledge.

Being a trained and experienced professional, whether as a doctor, nurse, or scientist in your home country, is no guarantee that you will be able to find a job at the same level upon coming to America. Speaking and understanding English well is essential, especially because medical specialists are entrusted with people's lives. You want to make sure that you can understand and explain the procedures you are using to others who, for instance, may be helping you in the emergency room. Medicine is one area in which you cannot take a communication risk.

Service and skilled labor jobs

Service jobs are booming as the population all over America is growing. Restaurants and hotels are in dire need of personnel in management, human resources, and as executive chefs—to name just a few positions. However, if you have never worked in a service environment, in order to move up to more prestigious and better-paying positions, you might have to start at entry level and prove that you are a quick learner.

Some of the entry-level jobs in hotel/restaurants include reception/front desk clerks, housekeepers, busboys, waiters, dishwashers, kitchen help, and parking valets. To start, the pay may be minimal, and if you have other mouths to feed, you may not be able to provide for your family. This is sometimes why you hear of immigrants working two or three jobs. It may be physically exhausting, but you may not have a choice.

Because of rapid development in many major suburban areas, construction work or manual labor has significantly increased in the last few years. But because the economy is booming, builders and contractors find it difficult to hire carpenters, plumbers, roofers, and other help. These workers have the luxury of picking and choosing which work they want to accept. If you are a skilled worker, other builders and contractors may offer you more money to lure you away from their competitors.

In the last few years, many semiskilled and unskilled workers have entered the United States through the family preference visa program. These people are the ones working manual-labor jobs. As an immigrant, it is no longer a disadvantage if you do not have an advanced education, as long as you have usable skills that are in demand by service or construction-related businesses.

Apprenticeships

An apprentice is a beginner in a job. Apprenticeships—a popular way to learn by doing—may be available for some skilled labor jobs. Many vocational schools offer apprenticeship-like programs as part of a course. Apprenticeships are not practical in all fields and in large organizations because of logistical difficulties. It could be a nightmare trying to match the right master or expert (a highly skilled and experienced craftsman) with the right apprentice. Besides, the expert's time is extraordinarily valuable and it might be difficult, if not impossible, to take time away from an organization's immediate needs to supervise an apprentice.

In a way, mentors are advisors, coaches, or tutors who may play a role, but mentors are not the same as masters or experts. Mentors typically give general guidance, while experts usually give specific guidance in a particular trade or vocation. Although companies may have mentoring programs and may assign you a mentor, advice is likely to be limited to career issues.

Temporary and seasonal jobs

Christmas and summer are times when temporary and seasonal jobs are most plentiful. Children of immigrants (high school and college students) often look for seasonal or temporary jobs because special skills are not usually required.

Sometimes, stay-at-home moms are also out looking for seasonal jobs to earn extra money for Christmas. They can work nights once their spouses are home from their own jobs. During the Christmas season, you can find immigrant women and teenagers working at department stores as cashiers, gift wrappers, stockers, and other jobs that do not require extensive communication with customers. Often, it is enough for them to understand basic English.

Finding Employment

Finding a job in America can be challenging because you have many sources to tap into, such as classified ads, the Internet, job fairs, or networking. You can also use employment agencies to do the work for you, but remember that reputable agencies do not charge upfront fees to job seekers.

If you are already in America, you may be overcautious when looking for a job for the first time. Even with extensive experience in your area of expertise in your home country, you may worry because the expectations of companies in America can be a lot higher than in your home country.

Chung K. Pak knows what problems immigrants face when seeking employment, so he initiated a community group whose main purpose is to help people from various ethnic groups to find employment.

Chung extends his help further by providing free training and seminars that teach interview skills, preparing résumés, cover letters, and thank-you letters. Chung has a network of professionals who volunteer their time to help him. His seminars include presentations on "how to handle job interviews," and include conducting "mock interviews." According to Chung, "Looking for a job the first time makes people new to the country anxious. Many people who come for help want to ensure that they know how to answer an interviewer's questions intelligently."

Processes and sources to find employment vary. Years ago, the practice was to send a formal application letter with a well-prepared résumé printed on expensive paper. But since the 1990s, sending formal applications and résumés by mail is just one process, and is often considered passé. Employers now accept faxed applications and electronic résumés sent over the Internet. Progress has caught up with us. Almost everything now is faster.

If you have access to the Internet, you can simply use the mouse to do your job hunting. The Internet is a useful tool for seeking jobs because you can access different sites that allow you to check vacancies. If you do not have a computer at home, many libraries offer computers with free Internet access. You can sign up for computer use and are usually allowed one hour to use the system.

If you are a student, many schools have resource rooms with computers you can use to look for part-time jobs. In addition to computers in schools and libraries, you can also rent computers for a reasonable fee at "cyber cafés" and at some large shopping malls. Another option is to find a friend who owns a computer and ask if you can use it for a few hours to look for a job.

There are many resources for finding jobs, including classified advertisements that appear in daily newspapers. In a more personal but direct way, you can network with people in your field and take advantage of word-of-mouth referrals and personal recommendations.

Job fairs are becoming popular now because employers can reach many applicants at one time and can even interview candidates for job openings. Many hotels use job fairs to advertise their job openings. They make announcements in major newspapers to inform job seekers where the job fair will be and maintain a booth at the fair where they can accept résumés and interview potential employees.

Of course, you can also go directly to the Web sites of specific companies and check advertised job opportunities. Some companies that have Web sites allow you to send your résumé electronically. You can also research career opportunities from articles, company profiles, classified ads, and an executive recruiter directory. Similar to *Career Magazine* is the NationJob On-line Jobs Database, which includes specialty pages on computer software and systems, education, science and technical fields, and many more.

People I interviewed who had completed graduate and doctoral programs found work in their fields of study. Those who preferred to work in service-oriented jobs are satisfied with the work they do, too, although their current jobs were not part of their original plans. Many of their plans evolved due to necessity or change in career interests. Sam Quaye wanted to be his own boss, and Henry Tse, a waiter, only wanted to save enough money so he could go home to Hong Kong to start a business. Christina Bonnell was frustrated in a job that she held for many years. Her solution was to change careers—from human resources to real estate.

Julio Sasaki completed his studies and was tempted to go home to Peru but his mother convinced him to stay in America for "career advancement." Julio knew that if he had gone home and accepted any job, it would have been a step down. Other than teaching, there were not any real opportunities to find a good-paying job commensurate with his skills. Although it took a while, Julio found a job that matched his qualifications.

Ravi Sahay had a better experience seeking employment. When he arrived in America in 1971, he was already a green card holder, although his original purpose was to study. After completing his advanced degree in engineering at City College in New York and an MBA degree at the University of Rochester, his goal shifted in another direction, from working in a corporation to becoming an independent consultant.

When he was twenty-three years old, Ravi was able to get his first job as a mail clerk for $62 a week, collecting mail and running errands. Ravi got this job in an architectural company through a job placement agency by replacing a fellow immigrant. "If you had seen me arrive for my interview," he said, "you would have thought that I was applying for an executive job because I was dressed to a tee. To tell you honestly, I was overdressed."

Ravi did not stay long in that job. He got another job interview through a classified advertisement in a New York newspaper. Xerox was looking for a high school graduate to work as a technical representative in Manhattan. "That was obviously a job beneath my qualifications, but I took the tests, got an interview, and was offered the job in two months. I told myself that a job as a technical representative is nowhere close to an engineering job, which I was aiming for, but since I was still going to graduate school everything else was secondary. That job helped me know more about America and make friends. It also gave me a very good understanding of Xerox machines and an ability to talk comfortably to customers. This sharpened my ability to speak English. Although I had a very heavy accent, it was not a barrier."

The hidden job market

Another source of employment opportunities is the hidden job market (companies with unadvertised job vacancies) where you may find good jobs that are never advertised. It just takes effort and patience to do the research and networking. You will find these unadvertised jobs by networking with your friends, members of clubs or associations you belong to, or by hiring a headhunter who has access to these jobs.

In terms of networking, the hidden job market can also be reached through people who know of openings, plans, and employer needs. Sources for employment are endless. It is a matter of patience and perseverance. Could the hidden job market work for you? It could work for anyone who has the right qualifications and experience. With a lot of hard work and effort, you can find good opportunities for professional jobs.

Other than job search Web sites, you can also engage employment agencies. Most reputable agencies do not charge fees to job seekers, but it would be wise to ask the employment agencies that you plan to engage who pays for the fees. Appendix D, *Business and Employment Resources,* includes a list of agencies that recruit people for various types of positions in various industries.

Preparing a résumé

A résumé is a selling tool that outlines your skills and experiences so an employer can see, at a glance, how you can contribute to the employer's business. You want the most effective résumé that speaks about you, is clearly focused on a specific job, and addresses the employer's stated needs for the position.

If you have gaps in employment, make sure you explain the reasons for these gaps, which could be that you went back to school to update your knowledge and skills. Explain. You should describe your degree and course titles in terms familiar to the employer if the title of the degree or course is not common in America.

If you want to create a résumé but need information on how to do it, many books are available to help. A good book is *High Impact Résumés and Letters: How to Communicate Your Qualifications to Employers* by Ronald L. Krannich, January 1998, Impact Publications, ISBN: 1570230854. Price: $19.95.

You can also find information on how to create a résumé through the Internet. For instance, look up *www.jobstar.org*. If you are a student, you can visit your school's guidance and placement center for help with preparation of a résumé. For additional information, see the sample résumés in Appendix D, *Business and Employment Resources.*

Preparing for Job Interviews

When you are scheduled for a job interview, it is natural to get nervous, especially if it is your first job interview in America. When asked a question, pause for a moment to gather your thoughts and then respond to the interviewer's question calmly, with confidence. Think about the country you are coming from and how this might differ culturally when seeking a job. If you come from Asia, for instance, you may not be comfortable looking at the interviewer directly, but you should practice doing so. Learn as much as possible about the job you apply for, even stretching yourself to think about "situational" questions.

Preparation is important before any job interview. Practice interviewing before a video camera, with a friend playing the interviewer. Study the company's annual report so you can better handle questions that test your knowledge of the company. (You can obtain annual reports for public companies from most libraries.) In addition, if you have a friend who works for the company, talk to him or her to learn more about the company. Most important, read some of the books that teach job interviewing skills and list common interview questions.

Do not be overcautious, because you cannot be expected to always know everything. Interviewers normally ask standard questions about previous jobs, interests, accomplishments, and so on.

One thing that you should never do is apologize if you are not sure of your answers. What is there to apologize for? Just do the best you can and respond to questions confidently without pausing. Many times this works well because your body language will show that you are thinking.

Finally, believe in yourself and try to do your best. If you lack self-confidence, ask advice from friends or relatives who have had extensive experience going for interviews.

Legal issues pertaining to job interviews

Because interviews are used as selection tools, interviewers must be careful that the questions they ask comply with federal laws and regulations pertaining to hiring. Two of the most relevant pieces of employment legislation are the Civil Rights Act of 1964 and the Americans with Disabilities Act (1992).

Civil Rights Act of 1964

Title VII of the Civil Rights Act of 1964 is the principal body of federal legislation in the area of fair employment. According to Title VII, it is unlawful for an employer to make hiring decisions based on race, color, religion, sex, or national origin.

Americans with Disabilities Act (ADA)
The ADA is a civil rights law for people with physical or mental disabilities and for some people who are treated as though they have these kinds of disabilities. According to the ADA, it is unlawful to discriminate against a "qualified individual with a disability" who can perform the "essential functions" of the job, with or without a "reasonable accommodation." Employers are not required to make an accommodation that would impose on them an "undue hardship."

Both pieces of employment legislation affect the types of questions that can be asked during an interview. As a general rule, the interviewer should ask only those questions that are clearly job-related and indicative of the candidate's experience and ability to perform the essential functions of the job.

Table 3 shows a list of sample legal and illegal interview questions.

Job Training

Once you are hired, you should continue to learn new skills and relearn old ones. Training, like formal education, can be obtained in a number of ways. You can do it by self-study or by taking classes through your company or elsewhere at a vocational training center or community college, for example. Most large companies allocate training money for their employees. It is a great opportunity to keep your skills current.

Learning from others is also quite effective. Usually during your first few weeks you are given an orientation to learn about the company, your work environment, people you will work with, and the projects you will do. Most organizations now also have informal luncheons to share knowledge and help orient new employees. You can also learn information about your company during staff meetings and from informal meetings with your coworkers. Learning on the job can be done in many ways if you are resourceful and take pride in self-learning.

Table 3 – Legal vs. Illegal Interview Questions

Legal questions	Illegal questions
Which foreign languages you can read, write, or speak fluently IF the question is job-related	If you are a U.S. citizen
Whether you have a driver's license (if necessary for the job)	Your nationality, place of birth, parents' place of birth, how they came to learn to speak English
What your past work experiences have been	About your religion (e.g., name of your church or parish, which religious holidays you observe)
Whether you are willing to work any shift (if required for the job)	Your marital status
If you are willing to relocate	Which societies or associations you belong to
What future professional career plans you have	How many children you have, plan to have, or how they are cared for while you work
If your past or present employers may be contacted	What your spouse (if you are married) does for a living and how much he/she earns
If you are over eighteen years old	Whether you have ever been divorced
What your prior attendance record has been	Past or current substance abuse
If you can perform the essential job functions (with or without accommodation)	Questions directly concerning the existence, nature, or seriousness of your disability
	For a photograph as part of the application
	Whether you have worked under another name, the maiden name of your spouse or mother, or the full names of brothers, sisters, and extended family members
	Whether a candidate needs reasonable accommodation to perform the job—unless you have an obvious disability or have volunteered to disclose this information to the interviewer

Source: Web site: *www.homejobsplus.com.*

Green Cards and Employment

Immigrants who come as permanent residents or green card holders usually have few problems with the INS because they are allowed to work anywhere, anytime. Upon arrival in America, they can look for a job right away.

When Elena Minnitti received three years of postdoctoral training at Scripps Research Institute in San Diego, Scripps sponsored her for an H1-B visa, which allowed her to work only if she stayed employed with Scripps. To qualify for an H1-B visa, Elena first received a job offer from Scripps for duties to be performed in the United States. Her employer filed what is known as an "attestation" with the federal Department of Labor, which, among other things, certifies that the employer will be paying at least the average or "prevailing" wage for the type of job in that particular geographic area.

Employers are responsible for following the law no matter who they hire. Most companies ask that you complete a U.S. Department of Justice form called Employment Eligibility Verification. This permits the employer to verify your information with the INS. To be eligible to legally work in the United States, this form asks whether you are a citizen of the United States, a lawful permanent resident with alien number, or an alien authorized to work until a specific date. You also have to indicate your alien number or admission number. Other companies may ask for your green card, your passport, or your Social Security card.

Finding a job without local experience

Getting a job without local experience is a challenge in itself. Most large companies require that you have experience working in America so that they can easily check your references.

More often than not, you serve yourself well by accepting a job in a small company that does not require local job experience just to get your foot in the door. You can always find another job once you have gained enough experience.

Permanent residents who talked to me said that the length of time it took them to find a job depended on the type of job they were looking for, their education, and their previous job experience. That is why it took a few weeks for some and a few months for others. For them, it was not a matter of not being allowed to work, it was more about finding jobs quickly in companies that did not require local job experience.

Perseverance means addressing issues you have control over, like accepting a job that is less than what you expected while continuing to improve your skills and search for work that better matches your qualifications.

Students and tourists

On the other hand, non-immigrants, especially tourists who were not legally allowed to work in America but decided they wanted to work anyway, were in for a rude awakening. It was not easy. Hiring and retaining an immigration lawyer took money, and even if one had the money, there were no guarantees about getting a green card.

Non-immigrants who come on student visas are qualified to work under certain conditions. Immigration law states, "If you are given a job as part of the terms of a scholarship, fellowship, or assistantship, the job duties must be related to your field of study and no special work permission or application is required." This is true even when the job is located off-campus.

Succeeding at Work

Once you complete your job interviews and are lucky enough to be hired, you will be ready to use these tips on how to succeed at work:

Be visible. If you want to ensure that you move up the career ladder, be aware that you can play the same games as others do, such as being highly visible to top management and joining key task forces. Often, getting a promotion is more about who you know than what you know.

Share your accomplishments. Without bragging or being arrogant, let people know how good you are. Take responsibility for communicating with your managers, peers, and colleagues.

Take some risks. If you have prepared yourself well, take some risks too. This is actually a good sign that you can accept responsibilities that are more challenging and not just responsibilities you are comfortable with.

Develop a style managers are comfortable with. It is important to be yourself. If your style of working has worked well for you in previous jobs, do not change it. You should also find out the manager's style. This way, you can adjust, but not necessarily change your style completely.

Seek challenging assignments. Do not accept assignments because they are easy and you already know how to do them by heart. This attitude is limiting. To move up to management positions, you have to be willing and able to accept more difficult and challenging assignments. You are not expected to be perfect when working on difficult tasks for the first time, but you can learn from your mistakes and grow.

Find a mentor. Many large companies have mentoring programs. When you are a new hire and are still learning your way around the organization, effective managers may assign you a mentor who can help guide you and provide career advice.

Understand the company culture. Every company has its own culture that employees are expected to adhere to. You will find out early on what this culture is during job interviews, through your mentor, by attending a new employee orientation program, and simply by working in the company a while.

Take advantage of opportunities. You are responsible for your own career advancement. Although your manager can provide advice and support, you have to actively seek out opportunities through internal job vacancy postings and networking.

Balancing your work and personal life

It is important for you to accept that if you have to work two or three jobs, you may not find quality time to spend with your family. The personal time you have left may only be enough to get some sleep before you start the whole routine again the next day. You have to be emotionally prepared to handle this difficulty, especially if you are the sole provider. And in many cases, both spouses work more than one job, entrusting the care of younger children to older siblings. If you work long hours, you also might not have the opportunity to share meals with your whole family.

Children are usually resilient and should understand that you are working hard for their benefit. But you have to be emotionally ready to miss seeing them when you want to, and you have to spend quality time with them as the opportunities allow. I know many people who came to America with their children but with little money to provide for them. Pragmatic and honest about their status, they sat the children down and explained what was expected of them in terms of support. The parents knew what they were up against economically, and that it would not be easy, but being open and honest in discussing the issue with the older children was the best way to start. The older children understood that they needed to help with household chores (e.g., cooking and cleaning) and taking care of the younger siblings before and after school until the parents came home. Because of lack of education and the ability to speak English well, the parents could only get domestic-type jobs at meager salaries. Working two or three jobs was the only way they could afford to live decent lives.

4. Managing Your Finances

Managing your finances is a goal-oriented activity, which includes saving and putting your money to work. It means actively managing your financial affairs. If you are managing your personal financial affairs, it is a plan for you and your family's future. If you are managing financial affairs of your own business, you must plan for profitability.

The people I interviewed for this book were not comfortable talking with me about their finances. However, the majority work for large companies and told me that they participate in 401(k) plans and have investments in stocks and bonds.

Financial Planning

Financial planning means setting goals and procedures for using and saving money. Financial planning could be for personal or business purposes. Whether you are self-employed, own a business, or work for a company, it is wise that you plan well for the future and that you periodically update your plan as your situation or goals change. For instance, if you are single but have plans to get married and have a family, you may have to make adjustments in your finances in order to meet growing needs. This would include, for example, saving for your children's education.

For a list of books about personal finance, refer to Appendix C, *Budget, Finance, and Tax Resources.*

Banking

Many immigrants sell their property and bring all the money they have with them to start a new life in the United States. Some still have the habit of keeping their money at home, in boxes tucked under their beds or in a corner of their cupboards. But this habit is out of date for most people who are employed. Immigrants' attitudes of keeping money at home have changed significantly. Many now desire to put their money to work through investments, or through savings accounts where they can earn interest and see their money grow.

Saving money

Personal savings represent money set aside to cover future needs such as car repairs or emergency situations. Banks and savings and loan institutions offer savings accounts and certificates of deposits (CDs), which earn interest and are insured up to a certain limit by government institutions, such as the Federal Deposit Insurance Corporation (FDIC).

Borrowing money

If you start a business, buy a house, or get a consumer loan to buy furniture and fixtures, you may need to borrow from a bank or finance company. However, be forewarned that there have been scams associated with some smaller lenders, so be careful when you deal with them, as you should with any financial institution or advisor.

The type of loan you apply for is based on your ability to pay and your creditworthiness. If your credit is good, you may be able to obtain a signature or unsecured loan; otherwise, you may not have an alternative and will need to obtain a secured loan.

Signature loans and secured loans

Signature and secured loans are both obtained from banks. A *signature loan* is the simplest method of obtaining money quickly and conveniently. It is also called unsecured financing because the loans are made without any collateral or liens against an asset. The unsecured lender has no prior claim on your property as a borrower.

Signature loans can be made for terms as long as ten years and are generally granted to people or businesses that have demonstrated credit responsibility. Loans from $5,000 up to $100,000 can be obtained in this manner. Additional requirements and restrictions may be necessary on loans over $100,000.

Loan approval rests heavily on your employment history, personal credit rating, and ability to repay the loan. If your ability to pay is limited, you can support your loan with collateral, such as stocks, bonds, and certificates of deposit, or by a personal guarantee of another person with a higher credit rating.

A *secured loan* lets you borrow up to the value of an asset, such as the money in your savings account. Other things besides savings accounts can be security for a loan, such as a car or a house. Banks generally charge a lower interest rate for secured loans.

Choosing a bank

For day-to-day needs, once you start working and have money to save, you need to choose a bank. Following are some questions you should consider before choosing a bank.

- Is the bank conveniently located close to your home or office?
- How high are its charges compared to its competitors? For example, some banks do not charge fees on checking or savings accounts if you maintain a minimum balance. Other banks charge monthly service fees.
- Does the branch closest to you have a twenty-four-hour automatic teller machine for obtaining cash during odd hours?
- Is the bank's policy on loans more favorable to a depositor or a nondepositor?
- Are accounts at the bank insured by an agency of the federal government, such as the FDIC or the National Credit Union Administration?
- Does the bank have other services you would need to use regularly, such as wire transfers to your family back home?

In general, all banks are required to be federally guaranteed. Expect to see FDIC signs on the bank's door or windows.

Credit unions

Credit unions are a special kind of thrift institution created by people with a common bond. This common bond might be employment in the same company, membership in the same union, or residence in the same area. Credit unions offer financial services at lower costs than most banks. In the United States, there are approximately 13,000 credit unions, of which about 60 percent are federally chartered and about 40 percent are state chartered.

An advantage of banking with your company's credit union is that it typically offers slightly higher interest rates on regular savings accounts than savings and loan institutions and banks. Credit unions often offer free life insurance and lower interest rates on loans, compared to most commercial banks. You might also get a better rate if you decide to purchase a certificate of deposit.

Credit unions are excellent sources of loans for new and used cars, home improvements, and other major purchases. For convenience, you can usually repay your credit union loans by automatic deduction from your paycheck. If you are not good at keeping within your budget, this can help you set aside a portion of your salary.

Money market accounts

As you progress and are ready to start investing more, you can check the money market deposit accounts. These are especially designed for you to earn money market rates of interest if you do not want to tie up your funds in certificates of deposit (which are also known as savings certificates or term accounts). If you know you plan to withdraw cash frequently, a money market deposit account may be better for you than a certificates of deposit, where your funds are tied up for a specified period. And, depending on your bank's policy, you might have to pay a penalty for early withdrawal before the certificate of deposit matures.

Safe deposit boxes

If you have valuables, such as jewelry and negotiable bonds, you might think about getting a safe deposit box at your bank. Keeping everything in the same bank will be convenient for you.

Retirement Options

From the day you start working, setting money aside for retirement is a serious consideration. Large companies typically offer several retirement options. Since you may work for several companies in your lifetime, you can "roll over" your retirement money so that it's kept intact until you are ready to retire. You should plan and ensure that you have a strategy that will allow you to enjoy spending the money you have saved without constantly worrying about running out of money too quickly.

Working for large rather than small companies generally has advantages because you are usually given options to put your money into a 401(k) or other interest-generating retirement fund. Being self-employed also gives you advantages of investing in Keogh plans and SEP-IRAs.

Social Security

Each time you receive a paycheck, a portion of your income is withheld for payment into the Social Security system. Your employer contributes an equal portion. Part of that money goes toward Social Security benefits and a smaller portion toward Medicare. If you are self-employed, you pay the entire amount toward Medicare. If you are self-employed, you pay both your contribution and that of your "employer." A recent change in the Social Security provisions allows you to continue to work and receive full Social Security retirement benefits at the same time.

Retirement plans

Following are descriptions of common retirement plans:[6]

401(k). A 401(k) is a qualified, tax-deferred retirement plan offered by employers, which allows employees to save a percentage of their salary for retirement. Employers often match 401(k) contributions, either in whole or in part. Most 401(k) plans permit you to contribute a fixed percentage of your before-tax pay, usually between 1 and 15 percent. Tax law limits salary deferrals, which are adjusted periodically for inflation.

Some plans also allow you to make additional after-tax contributions. Before-tax 401(k) contributions are not subject to federal income tax until you withdraw money from the plan. At that time, you will be taxed on the full amount of the withdrawal at ordinary income-tax rates (currently as high as 39.6 percent). However, when you withdraw money at the time of retirement, your income may be low enough to make the tax consequences minimal. You may also be subject to an early withdrawal penalty on amounts taken out of the plan before age 59½.

Keogh. A Keogh plan is a tax-advantaged retirement plan that a self-employed person can establish for his or her benefit. The self-employed, for this purpose, include sole proprietors, partners, or incorporated entities and unincorporated professionals. If you are an owner (or part owner) of an unincorporated professional business or you work as an unincorporated professional person, you can take advantage of the ability to set up your own retirement plan.

If you pay self-employment tax under the federal Social Security system, you are most likely eligible to participate in a Keogh plan. If you have employees who are over age twenty-one and have been with you for more than one year of service, or work more than 1,000 hours in a year, they must be included in the plan as well. But your contributions on their behalf do not have to be as large as the ones you make for yourself. Any contributions you make for them are tax deductible to you. When you leave a job in which you have been part of an investment program such as a 401(k) plan, you must decide whether you want to take your money in lump sum or leave it in a retirement account, or "annuitize" it, where the money will be paid out to you in regular installments. You can have your company set up an installment plan, or you can buy an annuity. The decisions you have to make are many. You might consult a financial planner who can explain the retirement alternatives to you and help you understand the rules and options.

Individual Retirement Accounts (IRAs)

Individual Retirement Accounts are arrangements that allow you to save money for retirement in a tax-advantaged manner. An IRA is an account, not an investment. The money you put into an IRA could be held in the form of stocks, CDs, mutual funds, cash, bonds—just about anything, except options and other derivatives.

SEP-IRA. A SEP-IRA (Simplified Employee Pension Individual Retirement Account) is the easiest retirement plan to set up and maintain. You can establish a SEP if you earn self-employment income, regardless of whether you have employees. If you have employees, you are not required to offer them a SEP. As with an IRA, the plan's earnings are not taxed until you withdraw the money at retirement. All of the money contributed to your account immediately belongs to you. This means there is no mandatory minimum vesting period. In addition, you "guide" the investment. For example, if the contributions are invested in mutual funds, you can choose the fund(s) in which to invest your contributions.

Roth Individual Retirement Account (IRA) is the most popularly recognized option resulting from the Taxpayer Relief Act of 1997. The Roth IRA goes one step further than the regular IRA does by allowing your contributions to grow tax-free. It also outlines rules regarding contributions and withdrawals. Unlike regular IRAs, contributions to a Roth IRA are not deductible; however, depending on your age and other factors, the Roth IRA can offset the lost deduction by avoiding the income tax you would ordinarily pay on the compounded earnings of the account over its lifetime.

A "rollover" is a transfer of your money from a tax-qualified pension, profit-sharing, or other retirement plan to an Individual Retirement Account (IRA) or other qualified plan, which you might have occasion to do when you change jobs. The "rollover" must be made within 60 days after you receive this money. When you roll over an eligible distribution to an IRA or other qualified plan that accepts rollovers, you continue to shelter your money from income taxes. You are not taxed until you withdraw your funds from the rollover IRA or other plans. You also defer taxes due on the investment earnings on the amount rolled over.

Investments

Investment is the act of using money or capital to gain interest or income.

Many powerful investment opportunities are available as long as you have the money. If you are a paycheck-to-paycheck person, your money is typically spent on household expenses, such as food, clothes, utilities, rent or mortgage payment, car, and other needs. This means there is no money left to invest.

But if you have the money and are ready to invest, you have to make careful choices by putting your money to work safely and effectively, instead of spending it on nonessential items.

Putting your money to work

Charles J. Givens, the author of *More Wealth Without Risks*, said, "There are two approaches to investing—putting your money to work, and putting other people's money to work." [7]

Putting your money to work means investing. Some of the more common and familiar investments include:

- **Bonds.** Bonds are a debt instrument of an issuer (essentially an I.O.U. for money you lend to the issuer) that promises to pay you a specified amount of interest, for a specified time, with principal to be repaid on the maturity date.
- **Certificates of deposit (CDs).** CDs are FDIC-insured savings accounts offered by banks and savings and loan institutions. As with bonds, CDs are usually opened with a single deposit, earn a fixed return, and have a set maturity date. Their maturities usually range from three months to five years.
- **Mutual funds.** Investment companies that offer mutual funds enable their shareholders to pool their funds to be professionally managed as a single investment account.
- **Stocks.** Stocks represent ownership in a company. The value of a stock will fluctuate with the company's performance and the stock market in general.

Putting other people's money to work could include borrowing money for your business, investing in leveraged limited partnerships, borrowing the equity on your home to reinvest—just to name a few.

Taxes

Taxes are part of earning income whether you are self-employed, own a business, or work for a company. If you earn money, you must pay taxes. The amount you pay depends on how much you earn. You can deduct personal exemptions depending on your situation. When you are employed, a percentage of your income is deducted from your gross pay for income taxes.

Bella Morin works for an international organization and therefore has a G-4 visa. Under this visa, she is exempt from paying taxes as an expatriate. This immunity gives her an advantage over people who work for organizations with taxable incomes. Bella's spouse files a joint return indicating Bella's income as tax-exempt.

Tax forms

Federal tax laws and regulations are extremely complicated. But if you cannot afford to hire an accountant, it is possible for you to obtain the necessary documents and prepare your own income tax returns. Some of the most important forms include:

Form W-4. The U.S. income tax system is a pay-as-you-go system. In other words, you are expected to pay income taxes on your income as you earn it. If you have a fulltime job, you fill out a W-4 form to determine how much of your salary should be withheld in taxes. Your employer sends the appropriate amount to the government, the Internal Revenue Service. The W-4 form has worksheets to help you figure the amount that should be withheld.

Form 1040-ES. This is an estimated tax form. If not enough money is withheld from your salary because you earn extra income, or if you are self-employed, this form, which you file on the 15th of April, June, September, and January, lets you estimate the amount of tax you owe. You send an estimated tax payment with the form. Making insufficient payments can result in heavy penalties.

Form W-2. Your employer should send this form to you every January. It lists all the federal taxes you paid during the year as well as state and local taxes that were withheld from your pay. Check it carefully for accuracy and file it with your tax return.

Form 1040. This is the master form you complete when you file your tax return. You could be required to file any number of additional forms and schedules depending on your sources of additional income and deductions. 1040EZ and 1040A are shorter versions of 1040 for less-complicated returns. Every year, the Internal Revenue Service (IRS) sends packages to taxpayers, complete with the most used forms and preprinted mailing labels. If you do not receive one, you can get tax forms at banks, post offices, or regional IRS offices.

Types of taxes

Paying taxes is common everywhere. The rules and laws and the types of taxes may differ, but you pay taxes nonetheless. You might pay property taxes, depending on the property you own, and state income taxes depending on the state you live in, and you must pay federal income and Social Security taxes. You also usually pay sales and local taxes. Is there a penalty for not paying? Of course. Can you hide from the Internal Revenue Service? Not really. If you work for companies, taxes are automatically deducted from your paychecks. Loopholes may be possible for business owners and for the rich, but realistically, there is nowhere to hide. People fear the consequences: paying fines or going to jail.

The reality is that no one has the right to evade taxes, especially in America. Taxes are enforceable—not voluntary—contributions. Taxes can be overwhelming since you have to pay many different kinds. Once you earn money, you have to bear your share of paying for the federal, state, city, and county services everyone receives. In some states, such as North Carolina, you also are required to pay personal property taxes for each car you own, where the amount you pay is calculated based on the "blue book" value of your car. Naturally, the newer and more expensive the car, the higher the taxes you pay.

Deductions

Deductions are expenses you can claim to reduce your taxable income. Common deductions include qualified charitable contributions and student loan interest payments. Qualified charitable contributions are deductible if you itemize your deductions. For student loan interest payments, you can claim up to $2,000 (the amount changes every year) of student loan interest per year for the first five years, even if you do not itemize. Remember, tax deduction limits change every year. For more information on tax deductions, you can call or visit your local IRS office or access Web sites such as *www.taxplanet.com.*

You can get additional tax breaks if you are self-employed or own a business. Examples of deductions that people often overlook are paying off debt with a home equity loan rather than credit cards, and contributing old clothes, furniture, and other items to charity.

Other common deductions include the following:

- Job search expenses such as résumés, phone calls, postage, travel costs, and any other expenses related to your attempt to get a new job.
- Investment expenses such as investment publications, payment for investment advice, calls to your broker, and any other expenses related to the production of investment income.

- Supplies you use if you own a business. For example, as a writer, my computer and the cost of Internet access are deductible because I use them in my business.
- Tax planning advice. Anyone in business for himself / herself can deduct legal and accounting fees. If you are self-employed, tax preparation fees can be deducted as a business expense.

Standard vs. itemized deductions

Tax deductions fall into two categories: a standard deduction and an itemized deduction. A *standard deduction* is a simple tool that avoids the necessity of accounting for modest amounts or some minor expenses during the year that are not enough to merit listing one-by-one. If your deductible expenses add up to more than the standard deduction, you may itemize your deductions. An *itemized deduction* is all amounts you paid during the year for certain items, such as medical and dental care, state and local income taxes, real estate taxes, home mortgage interest, and gifts to charity.

Preparing tax returns

Completing and filing tax returns takes experience. If you are filing taxes for the first time and you do not know how to complete the forms, you might consider seeking help from a service such as H&R Block or a local CPA (Certified Public Accountant). However, if you are computer savvy and understand English well, you can purchase tax preparation software, such as TurboTax, and prepare the returns yourself. (More information on tax software can be found in Appendix C, *Budget, Finance, and Tax Resources.*)

Tax filing

Choosing the correct filing status is very important. Married filers should keep in mind that filing status depends partially on residency status. As a general rule, a resident and a nonresident cannot file a joint or combined return.

Be aware that Congress continually makes changes to the tax laws, so be sure you follow the guidelines for filing that are updated for the current year.

Joint filing. A joint return is the filing status for legally married people. This is usually, but not always, cheaper than filing separate returns. You and your spouse may file a joint state return only if you filed a joint federal return.

Separate filing. A separate filing is the filing status for people who are single or are married but filing a separate return. You are considered single if you are unmarried, or if you are divorced or legally separated under a separate maintenance decree.

Deadlines for tax filing

Personal income tax returns are due on April 15th. If the 15th falls on a weekend, the next business day becomes the due date. If you cannot meet the deadline, you can file a form to request an automatic extension. The IRS will grant a four-month extension, which runs out in mid-August. If you do not see any way you will be able to finish your return by mid-August, you can request an additional two-month extension, which allows you to file as late as mid-October. But you will have to come up with a good reason why you need extra time. You also have to pay the estimated amount of the taxes due at the time you request the extension.

5. Starting and Running a Business

Starting a business is much like creating a blueprint for a house you are building. You have to have each piece together to complete a whole. What type of business do you want to have? What plans do you need to put together? How much money do you need? What kinds of people do you need to hire to manage the business if you are not managing it yourself entirely? You need a well-thought-out plan that has all the details in place. You want to ensure that your structure is laid out properly and accurately before you open the doors to the public.

Running a business follows the structure that you carefully laid out. How will you operate it every day? Should you revisit your business plan in case something needs changing? How is your cash flow, both in and out? Are the people you hire the most appropriate to serve you well in your business? Much effort is put forth in both starting and running a business. You have to have what it takes to keep it going and succeed.

The people I interviewed who started their own businesses used different techniques to get going, like networking and getting advice from successful business people. They sought funding from formal sources (banks), and through informal approaches (pooling of resources like *kye* or borrowing from family and friends).

Starting Your Own Business

Starting your own business is a major undertaking. It is about preparation and planning, money, risks and returns, budgeting, and leveraging your capital structure. To get started, you may borrow money or recruit investors to finance your business. You also must make decisions about managing your debt and investing your time wisely. You must learn to be creative because running a business is not an easy feat.

Dave Lang came to America as a refugee in 1975 together with his whole family, six brothers and sisters and his parents. For twenty years, Dave worked mostly in retail sales in different cities starting in Kansas, and then moving to Chicago, Houston, and Atlanta. Since he was a child, he dreamed about owning his own business. Although he did not finish college, he took some general business management courses at a community college. At that time, Dave did not know what type of business he wanted to get into. All he wanted to do was make money.

However, it was not until 1995 when he moved to Virginia from Atlanta that he started his own business. Because of lack of capital, he almost gave up hope of starting his business. But then his luck changed. He met several Vietnamese people who asked him if he wanted to open a nail salon business. A spot opened up in Ashburn, Virginia. A partner put up half of the money. Dave needed only $15,000, which he borrowed from his mother. Dave eventually bought out his partner in 1999 and he is happy to be a sole proprietor.

When Dave's nail salon opened in 1995, he found nail technicians through word-of-mouth referrals and personal references. He hired only Vietnamese, not by choice but because they were highly recommended to him by a friend who owns a nail salon in Tysons Corner, Virginia. Dave also knew that few native-born Americans would work in his business because the pay was meager. Nail technicians work by commission per service (50 percent if you are new or inexperienced and 60 percent if you are experienced), but with no benefits.

Dave's business started small, with only two or three nail technicians. He had to build his clientele first before he decided to hire more people. With his generosity, flexibility, and focus on customer satisfaction and customer service, the number of regular clients increased tremendously.

Because Dave recouped his investment within one year of starting his business, he is planning to open another nail salon. Nail salons are sprouting everywhere now, so he wants to make sure that he finds a location that is either inside a mall or in a densely populated city where he can be assured of more customers.

Louis Cheng came to America in 1971 from Taiwan and now owns two successful restaurants. He came on a tourist visa, got married soon after to his Taiwanese girlfriend, and eventually got his green card.

When Louis arrived in America, he stayed with friends temporarily, because they were willing to accommodate him for only a few weeks. With no money, Louis' only alternative was to go out and aggressively look for any job. Hungry and cold, he walked the streets in Chinatown in Washington, DC. Through sheer perseverance, he persuaded the owner of a small Chinese restaurant to hire him as a waiter. The job was arduous and the hours long, but Louis persevered, saved money, and is now financially independent.

Louis had set high but realistic goals for himself, knowing what he was up against from the outset. Although the road was not easy for him and he had to struggle for years, nothing could stop him. He kept going, moving from job to job to earn money and to learn different skills. He knew that he wanted to have his own business. That opportunity finally came in the mid-1980s. He had the expertise, the experience and the courage he needed, and he honestly believed he could now move forward.

With advice from family, friends, future partners, and investors, he told himself, "I am ready, Let me start my business plan." He traveled all over the local area to find the best location for the restaurant. Louis finally found a location where there were no other posh Chinese restaurants, although there were several carryout and cafeteria-style places that served Chinese food. Louis was unperturbed. He knew that his clientele would be different and more upscale. He did it, and now he is set for life.

In all the years that Louis has owned two restaurants, he has not changed since he set foot in America, other than becoming successful. He remains low-key, soft-spoken, and kindhearted. He has not forgotten his past and credits his current success to strong determination and patience. Even with success, Louis does not take things for granted. He still works hard and puts in long hours because he loves what he does.

Business Plans

Proper planning for your business—financial, operational, marketing, managerial—is the key to turning your idea into reality.

What vision do you have for your business? What are your objectives and long-term goals? To implement your vision, it is important to take the time to put your thoughts and intentions down on paper. You do this by creating a work plan, otherwise known as a business plan.

What is a business plan? It is a written summary of what you hope to accomplish by being in business and how you intend to organize your resources to meet your goals. In other words, a business plan describes the questions who, what, when, where, why, how, and how much that make your business idea come to life in your mind.

Your business plan will help you anticipate important decisions because it performs three functions:

The *first and primary function* is that it forces you to think through each aspect of your business, especially since you will face many decisions during the first few months before you open your business.

The *second function* is that it allows you to have a "test" before you actually open your business. It exposes you to financing requirements, personnel, profits, and problems. It also simulates what you can expect in the early months and years of operation.

The *third function* is as a sales tool for potential investors. If your plan shows that you are familiar with every aspect of your business, you will be more self-confident and better able to attract investors.

Business plans are often crucial when it comes to borrowing large amounts of money, since many lenders will want to see one.

Planning and good management skills are vital to your business success. If you do not plan, you run a very high risk of failure. If you do not know where you are going in your business life, there is little chance that you will get to where you want to be.

Preparing a business plan

It is not easy to write a business plan if you have not done one before. Your plan must reflect your strategies and ultimate goals.

There is nothing mysterious about preparing a business plan. You may require the assistance of an accountant, a lawyer, or another advisor or businessperson. Ultimately, however, the plan should reflect your own thinking—you need to go through the thought process of understanding and planning for all aspects of your business. It is an important term of reference for you at the outset and on an ongoing basis in the future. Remember, business planning is a continuous process.

You can create your own plan from scratch, hire a consultant to create one for you, or use software designed especially for creating business plans. Following are some tips for preparing a business plan:

- Get straight to the point.
- Be concise about where you want to take your idea and how you will achieve your goals. Keep it brief.
- Use tables, charts, graphs, and illustrations as necessary.
- Explain and substantiate any assumptions you make about future income, annual revenue, and their sources. Establish realistic break-even points.
- Use the body of the plan to tell the basic facts and include appendices for details such as financial statements.
- Package it professionally: neatly typed, proofread and securely bound.

Remember that a business plan is a working document—revisit it regularly, use it to monitor your business' progress and revise it periodically.

Following is an outline of a formal business plan:

The Cover Sheet (the title of your plan)
The cover sheet should contain the name, address, and telephone number of the business and the names, addresses, and phone numbers of all owners or corporate officers (or if you are a sole proprietor, your information). It should also tell who prepared the business plan and when the plan was prepared or revised. To help

you keep track of copies you send to lenders and prospective investors, mark each cover sheet with a copy number.

Executive Summary
The executive summary summarizes your plan and states your objectives. If you are seeking loan funds or investment capital, it will list your capital needs, how you intend to use the money, and how you intend to repay the loan or return profits to the investor. While you are writing your plan, many previous ideas will change and new ideas will develop. Therefore, the executive summary is most effectively formulated after writing your plan. This section should be concise and no longer than one page.

Table of Contents
Having a table of contents will help the reader move smoothly from one section of the plan to another when verifying information. For example, if a lender is reading financial information regarding advertising on a pro-forma cash flow statement, he or she can use the table of contents to locate the section on advertising to see how the money will be spent.

Organizational Plan (the first major section of your plan)
This section contains information on how your business is put together administratively. It includes such things as a description of your business, your legal structure, who your management and personnel will be, where you will locate, how you will do your accounting, what insurance you will have, and what security measures you will take to protect inventory and information.

The Marketing Plan (the second major section of your plan)
Your marketing plan will contain information on your total market with emphasis on your target market. You will include information on your target market and your competition. You will make such decisions as promotion of your product or services, pricing, timing of market entry, and where to locate if it's tied into your marketing. You will also examine current industry trends.

Financial Documents (the third major section of your plan)
Your financial documents will help translate the information in the first two sections of your plan into figures that can be used to analyze your business and make decisions for higher profitability.

Supporting Documents
This section will include: owner/manager, résumés, financial statements, articles of incorporation / partnership agreements, legal contracts, lease agreements, intellectual property (copyrights, trademarks, and patents), letters of reference, demographic data, and any other documents that are pertinent to support the plan.

Choosing the Type of Business

Business people I interviewed chose a business they had experience with, or a partner who already had experience in running a similar business.

Many immigrant entrepreneurs concentrate on service businesses such as nail salons, ethnic stores, and dry cleaning, because the amount of money they put up is much lower compared to franchises, such as McDonald's. And often, the more successful entrepreneurs sell their earlier businesses to new arrivals from their own countries.

Many entrepreneurial immigrants are more comfortable getting into service businesses because they may be required to speak only a little English. For instance, in the Vietnamese store I frequent the cashier speaks very little English but uses gestures to point customers to what they are looking for. And often, conversations are not necessary.

According to Dave Lang and Liklik Schroeder it is easier to start a service business compared to an information technology company or franchise that requires more investment up front. Service businesses are also easier to sell, and if you are in a financial bind, you may find it easier to recruit a partner.

Of the business people who talked to me, only Louis Cheng conducted market research before he opened his first restaurant. He said that the amount of investment was huge and he wanted to make sure there was a market for his restaurant in a county where the population was still growing. When Louis started, he was ambivalent because the population growth in his area was stagnant. But in a matter of two years after he opened his restaurant, construction of planned communities started sprouting. At that time, his restaurant was upscale compared to other Chinese restaurants in the area. Opening a second ethnic restaurant was easier because he conducted market research and because of his experience in starting and managing the first restaurant.

In contrast, Liklik Schroeder did not do market research because the business already existed. Liklik got into the vacuum cleaner business by virtue of marrying an American who already owned the business. Liklik worked at her husband's business before they even became friends. She was an outstanding salesperson, having gained experience dealing with people while working as a teller in commercial banks in the Philippines and in San Francisco. This became an asset that made her the top salesperson in the company she now co-owns. Liklik had no idea at the time she worked as a salesperson that she would one day fall in love and marry the owner of the company.

Liklik and her husband's business in Sacramento is growing exponentially. With already one hundred employees on their payroll, sales are increasing rapidly and orders are coming from all directions—not only from California but from other American states as well. Through word-of-mouth and personal recommendations from people who have bought top-scale vacuum cleaners from their store, the increase in sales has allowed both owners and employees to receive incentives, such as travel to Hawaii and Las Vegas. They also send out flyers as a cost-effective way to reach new customers in other states.

Resources for identifying business opportunities

Identifying business opportunities depends on the kind of business you want to engage in. You can search through business want ads and telephone directories and obtain ideas by visiting your local Chamber of Commerce. You can also search the Internet for lists of venture capitalists who have money to invest and are looking for people with ideas for new businesses.

Telephone directories

Every resident gets a copy of a telephone directory each year: yellow pages for business listings and white pages for residential (and selected business) listings. When you look at the yellow pages, you can find types of businesses you are looking for. It would be even easier if you know the name of a particular business and the city and state where it is located. Other than the yellow pages, you can also dial 411 for information from any city to find local or long distance phone numbers.

Chambers of Commerce
Your local Chamber of Commerce can be a great resource for learning more about businesses in your area. The United States Chamber of Commerce is a business federation representing companies, business associations, state and local chambers in the United States, and American Chambers of Commerce abroad. You can visit *www.uschamber.org* for information on local offices in your state and for international offices in other countries.

Financing Your Business

Running a business profitably takes more than just hard work. You need a positive cash flow every month that your business is in operation. Remember that profits you get regularly do not all belong to you. You have to plan for overhead, such as employee salaries and benefits, property leases, upkeep and maintenance of your place of business, and daily operating expenses. That is why most business owners hire accountants to maintain their books and periodically review their financial situation to help them anticipate cash needs.

There are several ways you might get money for your business: bank loans, outside investors, pooling of resources, and grants are common methods of financing a business. Another common method of financing for small businesses is borrowing from friends and family or using personal savings to finance your business.

Ravi Sahay became an independent consultant in 1989. To start his own management consulting practice, which focuses on marketing and technology, he used his personal savings and severance pay from a job he held for the previous four years.

Loans

Bank loans are a traditional funding source. Most bank loans are tied to interest rates and a timetable. When determining whether or not to give you a loan, commercial lenders, such as banks and credit unions, rely heavily on your income projections. However, unless you have established yourself by having a three- to five-year track record, it is likely that, in addition to your personal signature, a commercial lender will expect assets as collateral. Personal assets, such as a home, can also be used to secure some loans.

If you start a business, you may want to borrow from friends and relatives first. If this does not work and you have already tried borrowing from the bank, you may be able to refinance your primary residence and use the cash to set up your business. When starting a business, immigrants often resort to the pooling of resources. Borrowing from banks is usually a last resort. However, since ethnic-owned banks cater to their own ethnic groups, getting a loan can be easy.

Pooling of resources

In many countries, local businessmen help each other financially. The most popular way of getting financing in many countries in Southeast Asia is by participating in a community savings fund known as *kye* (pronounced key).

In a *kye* with ten members, the lead businessman would set an amount (e.g., $10,000), and the members would contribute proportionally ($1,000 each) every month for a ten-month period. At the beginning of the *kye*, the lead businessman can use either a lottery or voting among members to determine the order in which members get money. In a lottery, each member gets to pick a number from one to ten. Each number represents a month; for example, number one is February, two is March, and so on. The member who picks number one, gets $10,000 for that month, number two gets $10,000 in March, and so on. In the voting option, all members vote to determine who gets the money.

A similar form of pooling of resources in Vietnam is *hui,* which functions as an informal bank made up of a small group of businessmen who each invest $1,000 or so in a communal fund. That money is available for loans to members who want to start a business, and is normally paid in monthly installments.

Pooling of resources is not always successful. Sometimes it fails, because some could not put their money into it every month or because others ran off after collecting their money so they would not have to repay their loans. The leader is responsible for these failures.

Outside investors

Entrepreneurial immigrants who start businesses based on unique ideas or new products tend to seek money from outside investors. Generally, those who invest do not require monthly repayment like banks, because they receive part ownership of the business in exchange for their investment.

Michael Han,[8] a young Vietnamese American, financed his business in this manner. Han heads Golinq.com, a start-up technology company in Silicon Valley that provides e-commerce services based on a technology he created.

Han and his family escaped from Vietnam on a small wooden boat that his father built. It was a scary situation to be in. Rough seas. Storms. Pirates. Han's boat drifted for seven days and was without food and water for much of the time. Han's group was lucky to be rescued by a passing Norwegian ship and taken to Singapore, where thousands of refugees are taken.

Han's family found its way to the United States and settled in San Jose, California. Han went back to school and eventually received a graduate degree in engineering at the University of California at Davis. He was one of the few Vietnamese refugees who landed in Silicon Valley and began chasing the American dream.

Golinq.com is now international in scope and its success depends on having a large client base, much like any business. In the first two months, Han signed as clients four thousand small businesses all over the United States, and as far away as Africa and China.

Although pooling of resources to fund a business is common among Asians, Han did not use it. In a new economy take on this old-world practice, a respected group of Vietnamese investors in the San Jose area agreed to give Han $1.3 million to get his venture off the ground. Using *hui* is how the Vietnamese funded their businesses in the old days, but in a new interpretation of the rules of *hui,* all Han has to do in exchange for the money is to pay back the community by blazing a trail for other young Vietnamese entrepreneurs.

Many people are willing to invest in a business only if they believe the entrepreneur's idea will be extremely successful. Occasionally, friends and family members may invest in a business simply because they believe in their entrepreneurial relative and want to support his or her endeavors. A word to the wise in this case: These situations should be well thought out and properly documented. It is a good idea as well to include a buyout provision in your agreement with friends or family members. Avoid handshake agreements because they could lead to the end of your friendships if things do not go as planned. With a written agreement, if there are misunderstandings as the company progresses, you will be better prepared to settle them in a businesslike fashion.

Grants

What are grants? Grants are programs that cover a broad range of interests including academic and scientific research, publication support, travel and exchange programs, and many more.

Colleges and universities, nonprofit organizations, for-profit commercial organizations, state and local governments, and unaffiliated individuals are eligible to apply for grant funding.

Among the major types of grants are medical research, economic development, science and education.

As an example, the National Collegiate Inventors and Innovators Alliance (NCIIA) will award about $2 million in grants to faculty and students of member institutions through June 2002. Individual grants range from $2,000 to $50,000 and will be awarded to support the development, implementation, and institutionalization of new courses and programs in which student teams will develop innovative, entrepreneurial solutions to real-world problems. Funding can be used for course planning stipends (allowances) with a maximum of $2,000 for supplies, equipment, or expenses directly related to project development.

In medical grants, the Howard Hughes Medical Institute is committed to strengthening science education at all levels—from kindergarten through postgraduate training. In research grants, a new report from the American Cancer Society, Burroughs Wellcome Fund and Howard Hughes Medical Institute examines the training of biomedical scientists.

The Internet has many resources to find information about specific grants. You can access Web sites *www.nciia.org* and *www.lib.msu.edu*, which will provide you with comprehensive information about grants, databases, books, and other resources.

To apply for a grant, you must submit an application, which is specific and succinct. As an applicant, you must provide sufficient information to allow a foundation, such as the Fulbright Program, to clearly understand the objectives of the grant request and your qualifications.

All applications contain a summary sheet, which includes the following:

- Project title
- The applicant's name, address, telephone number, and e-mail address as well as principal participants in the project
- A concise abstract of the proposed project
- A specific amount (in U.S. dollars) sought from the foundation.

In addition to the summary sheet, applicants should supply the following:

- A **proposal**, which describes the purpose, audience, and product of the proposed project, and which addresses the applicant's relevant background and capacity to accomplish the task for which support is sought.
- A **résumé** of the principal participants.
- A **work plan** and **schedule** that include the applicant's plans for the distribution of the completed work.
- A **budget**, which includes various cost components of the total project and (if relevant) identifies other potential sources of support.
- Three **letters** from qualified references who are familiar with the ability and character of the applicant and are knowledgeable in the area of the proposal.

- Supplemental information, including photos, charts, and other graphics, when appropriate.

Managing Your Business

Ravi Sahay says doing business in America is quite different from doing business in India. Doing business in America is easier because of the availability of support through agencies such as the Small Business Administration. However, to be an entrepreneur, you need a considerable amount of reserve money in addition to emotional stability and skills; otherwise, it is a lonely and scary path.

Ravi's consulting business has changed in the past ten years. Initially, Ravi was doing reports on technology and business. Trends kept changing so he had to change his direction, too. To ensure that he was doing the right thing, Ravi consulted with a few companies at a high level to see how he could make money from the five patents he owned from copier/printer markets. Licensing the patents was an option Ravi looked at so that he does not have to consult forever.

Currently, Ravi works 40 percent of the time for a start-up company as a licensing consultant. He spends 30 percent of his time as a copier/printer consultant, 20 percent as a consultant on patents and licensing, and the remaining 10 percent working for nonprofit organizations.

Written contracts vs. handshake deals

In the age of complex business deals, written contracts are the norm. None of the immigrants I talked with support handshake deals, which are customary in many other countries. They said such deals are unrealistic and very dangerous. If you use a handshake deal and something goes wrong, there is no document as proof of what each person agreed on. It is about what you said and what he or she said. Who could be right or wrong? Both of you? There is no way to validate anything without documentation.

If you do business with your friends and family, you should create a written contract. Have the document notarized by a lawyer or at your bank with signatures from witnesses so that each person who is part of the contract understands the consequences of not abiding by the contract agreement. The written contract or guidelines between you and your friends and family should be as detailed as possible so no one misunderstands the other's intentions.

Another person I interviewed who also believes only in written agreements and signed contracts points out that even if you trust the people you hire to work for you, you can never be sure what kind of conflicts or disagreements might come up in your relationship. In order to keep your relationship intact, have a written contract to avoid disputes that may cause friction and destroy a valuable friendship. Of course, it is best not to hire your friends. But if you do, use a written versus an oral contract.

You may have heard about Max Fallek's old saying, "Don't mix business with pleasure." This is very relevant advice when you may be thinking about bringing friends into financial transactions regarding the business. But the truth is, just like family, friends can represent an excellent source of money needed for a small business start-up or to boost expansion of an ongoing business. You should exercise the same caution when dealing with friends as you would with people you don't know very well. Draw up a written contract. Do whatever you can to make sure the financial transaction will not result in lost friendships.

Hiring employees

Business owners and managers use different methods to hire employees for job vacancies. The most common is the daily newspaper help wanted ads. Other methods include personal recruiting at job fairs and college campuses, and word-of-mouth referrals. There is also reverse recruiting when job seekers advertise for a position wanted or post their résumés on job sites at various Web sites. Once the hiring manager has enough résumés to review, a "shortlist" of the most qualified potential employees is created.

Among the many contributors to this book, Louis Cheng, Dave Lang, and Liklik Schroeder have experience in hiring people. Techniques they used turned out to be appropriate since most of the people they hired years ago still work for them. Hiring people with the right skills that closely fit the job is a major factor, although other factors (e.g., positive attitude) come into play based on the company's specific needs.

Among the people who have hiring experience, Louis Cheng looks for good interpersonal and communication skills, Dave Lang looks for trustworthiness, while Liklik Schroeder looks for initiative and positive attitude.

Louis Cheng runs a people business, and when he hires employees he has to be convinced that they can talk to people politely and understand their needs. Louis cannot afford to hire people who do not have good people skills because his purpose is to ensure that customers keep coming back. In addition, through word-of-mouth from satisfied customers, Louis has the opportunity to get new customers.

Dave Lang is instinctive and hires only people he feels he can trust. In his business, his contractual agreements with each nail technician are verbal. He uses his intuition when making important decisions like contracts. He said that he would not resort to handshake deals if he could not trust the people who are seeking work in his nail salon. So far, his instincts have been right. Taking risks does not affect his personal decisions when it comes to hiring technicians, because Dave knows that conflicts cannot be avoided. Besides, he does not hire walk-ins who apply for jobs. All of his employees were from personal recommendations from friends who are in the nail salon business too. Dave said, "My situation is unique, but I have been lucky so far and I am confident that I will not anticipate personal conflicts as my business moves forward."

Liklik Schroeder is insightful and a good judge of character. Since profits made from the business come from sales of vacuum cleaners, Liklik ensures that she hires people who have experience selling, in addition to a positive attitude and initiative to find new customers. So far, her employees have not disappointed her.

Part II

Achieving Success

6. Strategies for Success

The people interviewed for this book achieved success in many different areas. Following are their stories and advice for personal and business success. They followed a variety of strategies, including setting goals and following a plan, learning English well, networking, taking risks, being persistent, staying flexible, expanding their horizons, finding support—and more.

Success takes practice and hard work. Getting it right often involves making mistakes, but mistakes are learning experiences. The whole point about challenge, surviving adversity, and working hard is to reach an end-goal, which is to achieve success. Success means more than just power and money. For many people, success also includes the self-satisfaction in knowing they worked hard to earn it. Success earned this way is much more meaningful and satisfying.

My own strategies for success are a mix of preparation and planning, hard work, patience, perseverance, courage, and not giving up until I have exhausted every option. For me, earning success the hard way is self-fulfilling. For instance, even with the challenge of being a novice writer, I looked at the road ahead and told myself I am going to make it.

General Strategies

What are strategies? Strategies are sets of decisions and actions for forming and implementing plans to achieve your goals. Strategies can be short-term or long-term. But for strategies to be meaningful, you need to focus on future-oriented actions. How will these strategies help you succeed in achieving your future plans?

Be well-prepared

Whatever job you pursue, it is important that you complete your education, be able to communicate well in English, have good interpersonal skills, understand and embrace the American culture, and continue to enhance your job skills. All these preparations will benefit you immeasurably in the long run. A contributor from China who did not want to be identified told me that preparation should not only involve processing paperwork, but also requires a solid education, job experience relevant to your field, good communication skills, and a good understanding of American history.

Elena Minnitti's preparation focused on coming to America as a postgraduate student:

> Before I came as a student, I spoke to people who had previously gone to study in the United States to find out how they did it. It was a laborious process. I scanned listings of U.S. schools to find out their requirements so I could prepare for them. I took the required exams—Graduate Record Exams (GRE), Test of English as a Foreign Language (TOEFL), and Test of Spoken English (TSE)—a year before I sent in applications to schools. Finally, two weeks before I actually left my country, I went to an orientation seminar sponsored by the U.S. Embassy. It gave me information about what to expect every step along the way: what to do from the moment you arrive at the U.S. airport and at the school, what the climate is like, what sort of clothes to bring or wear at different occasions, a general introduction to the people and culture, and so on.
>
> After I arrived at the university, the foreign office also provided an orientation about life on campus and survival tips, including: how to survive your first trip to Manhattan, what you should know before you take your first New York subway ride, etc. All this information has helped me tremendously, even to this day.

Have goals and a plan to achieve them

Why set goals? You set goals so you will know if you have achieved your plan. If you do not have goals, it is impossible to know where you are going, and how you are going to get there.

Do you set goals? Without question, it is imperative to create a schedule of goals. For instance, if you plan to have a family, a short-term goal may be to start saving money so that you are prepared for additional financial responsibilities, such as paying for your children's education. Effective goals are specific, measurable, time-limited and achievable, yet challenging.

Although it is important to put your goals on paper, to ensure that you fulfill them, you have to be disciplined enough to follow them.

Everything depends on your commitment, dedication, and a burning desire to succeed. Ask yourself: How important is this goal to me? Will I be satisfied if I forgo it? For example, Mike Ghanna, an Israeli, told me that his goal was to be his own boss because he did not want to work for others for the rest of his life. He achieved his goal after many years when he'd saved up enough money to start his limousine business. His business is now thriving and his next goal is to return permanently to Israel to live. His plan is in progress, starting with saving money so that by the time the children are grown he and his wife will be able to take the next step.

Bill Skea from the U.K. set a goal to complete a doctorate degree to ensure a much brighter career. Once he reached that goal, he worked in a variety of fulfilling jobs. In retrospect, Bill said that being goal-oriented, focused, persistent, and having a good education were the keys to his success.

Elena Minnitti also set goals. She emphasized, "Anyone who sets goals and dreams is tenacious. If you are determined and willing to work hard, you can achieve your goals."

Sam Quaye said that he did not give up on his goals and plans. He persevered even though his original plan to go back to school did not materialize. Sam's driving experience in America gave him the incentive to push further by owning and driving his own cab. Achieving a balance in his life gave him the flexibility to spend more time with his children.

I can add to these recommendations from fellow immigrants by saying that to learn and work with the system you need to be patient and persevere. Things you want to achieve do not come easily. You have to be well-prepared and keep your goals handy.

In my early years in America, determination, tenacity, and courage kept me afloat. Nothing was going to defeat me. Initially, I came as a tourist to stay for a month. But everything changed after I came. In the beginning, I had a clear goal to succeed and prove to myself and my family that with determination, tenacity, curiosity and stubbornness, I could make things happen.

My ultimate goal was to pursue advanced studies. It took several years to accomplish this because I wanted to take advantage of tuition aid programs. But once I got my degree, opportunities began to open up. One major opportunity was to work for Xerox Corporation in a job that closely matched my interests.

Achieving success is more than just having your goals in place. You have to know how to implement them. Keeping up and continuing to use the strategies and plans that you have in place will lead to success. Advice from successful people is worth listening to and learning from. After all, if they got there, you can, too.

Learn about American history

There are so many things to learn about America, the workings of the American government, civil rights, local and federal government (even at a high level), and so on. All these help you adjust and assimilate into the society. As Nilofer Qureshi, who originally came from Pakistan and moved to America to join her husband, said, "Learning about American history before coming to America is necessary because it helps you to transition into a new environment and a new culture."

Learn English well

You should be able to communicate and make friends regardless of your ethnicity, likes, dislikes, and viewpoints. As I emphasized in earlier chapters, being able to speak English well is critical if you want to be successful in America. To move up to a management position, you should be able to articulate your ideas clearly; if not, the train will pass you by. You may not get another opportunity immediately.

A contributor said, "If you speak little English, you will face one obstacle after another upon arriving in America. How will you inquire about potential job opportunities if you can't speak clearly? How will you respond to job interviewers' questions if you do not understand the questions? How can you apply for a job in your field if you cannot explain simple instructions to people you work with?" (For more information on learning English, refer to Chapter 2, *Getting the Right Education.*)

Get a good education

Having a good education is essential in today's world where competition for good jobs is keen. Because finding jobs has become competitive, job seekers with a good education may have an advantage over people who lack a good education.

Bella Morin's advice was, "If you have an opportunity and your company offers tuition aid programs, further your education if you want to advance in your chosen career." Elena Minnitti said, "It is important to have good grades to allow you an opportunity to apply for scholarships and further your education." Likewise, Maria Jaramillo, a retired teacher, added that you will be more competitive in obtaining a good job if you have a good education.

Take risks

You have to be gutsy to achieve your goals. If you are overcautious, you might not get where you want to go; or if you do get where you want to go, it will take you much longer. Anxiety and fear might stop you from making good judgments and quick decisions. For example, Louis Cheng and Dave Lang are businessmen who took risks when they started their businesses. They said that if you are extra careful and are afraid to take risks, you might miss an important opportunity.

Keep trying

You should not stop until you are confident that you have reached the goals you have set. If you stop trying, you sell yourself short. No one can help you if you don't first help yourself. Do not quit in the midst of adversity. Liklik Schroeder, a businesswoman from Sacramento, told me that it is not in her nature to quit. Quitting is giving up. It is a defeatist attitude. She gains by trying but loses if she gives up. Setbacks are simply a part of the road to success.

Elena Minnitti added her experience as a student:

> Being a student in America, alone and away from home, was one of the most trying experiences in my life. I had very little money. I was lonely, homesick, and had enormous pressure to do well in school. It was hard to concentrate. The courses were difficult. At the end of the first semester, I almost quit during the final exams. I forced myself to just keep slugging on. I told myself that if I fail my courses, the school would kick me out, my visa would expire automatically, and I would have no choice but to leave the country.

> Eventually I managed to pass all my courses. It did not end there, though. I still had four to five years of school ahead of me. Every semester I wondered whether it was time for me to quit and just get a job. Life would be so much easier. I would have more money, but I would not have my Ph.D. Each time I was ready to give up, I remembered something my former boss said to me: "When the going gets tough and all uphill, rest if you must, but do not quit." Therefore, I kept on trying. I am glad I did. With my degree, I get paid better; I have more opportunities for advancement, and more job benefits. All the hard work and sacrifice has paid off.

Be flexible

When you are in a new country, you might not be able to stick to what you were accustomed to in your home country. You have to be able to easily adjust or adapt to changes, whatever these may be.

Sometimes you do not have a choice but to be flexible if, for instance, your company is downsizing and your job is eliminated. To stay flexible, you should continue to learn new skills, so you can more easily find another job if yours is eliminated.

As an example, Lina Shoobridge, who is British and works for the International Monetary Fund on a G-4 visa, keeps an open mind. She said, "You have to change along with change. You cannot resist change because whether you like it or not, things will change without you. Flexibility is essential when you work and interact with other people."

Strategies for Personal Success

There are many important traits that helped the contributors to this book achieve personal success. Achieving success was not a matter of a single feat. Help from various supportive people (who had stakes in these individuals' successes) proved invaluable. The contributors enjoyed the benefits by rewarding themselves and the people who worked for them.

Reward yourself

Do not be too hard on yourself. When you have goals you want to reach, accomplish them one by one but do reward yourself to keep going. Rewards can come in many ways. It could be buying a new dress, dining out in a fancy restaurant, or relaxing at the beach. When you are in business, you not only reward yourself but also your employees who helped you make your business a success. Liklik Schroeder, a Filipino but now a naturalized U.S. citizen, said, "Employees are your most valuable asset, do not waste it. Giving bonuses or spending extra money for luxurious trips motivates your employees to work harder. A reward is a small price to pay for increased revenue."

Elena Minnitti loves to travel and the best rewards she ever gave herself were vacation trips. She told me:

> After a long hard semester in school, my friends (mostly classmates or roommates) and I would plan a trip somewhere in the United States or Canada. Since we were students and did not have much money, we often carried a sleeping bag and stayed with someone's relatives or shared hotel rooms. We drove a rental car and split the cost of everything. I saw a number of states this way. It taught me not only about U.S. geography and history but also how different life is on the East Coast, the West Coast, and in the Midwest. And it was fun!

Expand your horizons

It used to be that people worked for a company for many years, if not for a lifetime. However, with companies' trends of doing more with fewer people, having multiple competencies is a good strategy for staying employed. If you limit yourself to one area of specialty, you will be less marketable in the event the company you work for happens to downsize. Enhance your skills as often as possible whether on your own initiative or through support from your company. Be as open-minded as you can because this trait will help you achieve a better future.

Having a variety of skills has helped me to stay employed throughout the years. Also, I find being involved in a variety of endeavors more interesting than working in just one specialty. I enjoy exploring new areas, and am motivated by the challenges.

Find support

You cannot always do things alone. Find a support system, which could be a friend, a relative, a classmate, a colleague, or a mentor. You would be surprised how much other people's perspectives can help you see where you are in your plans. Often, when you are too close to what you are doing, you cannot see your progress. In this situation, Liklik Schroeder was lucky to get support from her mother and siblings already living in America. Through the family preference program, Liklik's mother sponsored the remaining siblings to join her in America. Her family's support system is solid and strong. Being a close-knit family surely helps.

Do not change who you are to fit into the mainstream

Let people accept you as you are and not what they want you to be. When you are in a new country, people may expect you to behave the way they do. Be able to adjust, but do not try to change yourself completely to do so.

For instance, Chung K. Pak wants to be appreciated as the person he is. He was in a work environment where some people adjusted their personalities to fit in. But he never relented. He was adamant that he was not going change his personality just to be appreciated. Throughout his career, he stood his ground and let his abilities speak for themselves. He said that he has enough ammunition (extensive educational background and experiences) to succeed.

Have self-respect and self-esteem

Self-esteem is very important. When you do not believe in your own abilities and sell yourself short all the time, that behavior will affect the way you work and the way you deal with people. If you lack self-esteem, other people will think less of you, even if you have much to offer. Second-guessing yourself or doubting your abilities will negatively affect your performance and credibility. Ellen Dimaano Latham, who originally migrated to Canada and moved to America after a few years said: "You have to respect yourself. Do not let yourself down and do not be intimidated by others. What helps tremendously is having spiritual strength. Trusting the Lord and believing in yourself and what you do will give you a special confidence that no one can take away."

Live a sensible life

When it is easy to get credit cards, you can easily overspend if you are not careful. Spend only what you can afford to and do not buy items when they are not needed. It is easy to fall into the credit card trap, especially when banks know you have a good credit history. Be forewarned: Once you start using credit cards, you might be tempted to use them again and again if you are not disciplined to stop.

Be kind to other people

You should always keep in mind that if you treat another person well, that person will treat you well in return. Use the "Golden Rule": "Do unto others what you want others to do unto you." Another contributor told me, "It does not matter whether you are a new arrival or have lived in America for many years, respecting others is a positive approach to life. You may not always get the same respect you give but, more often than not, when you treat people with respect you get respect back."

Continue to learn

Even if you have had education, training, and experience, if you really want to succeed, do not be satisfied with what you currently have. The job environment is getting increasingly competitive and workers are continuously improving. You do not want to be left behind. Elena Minnitti, Bharat and Ravi Sahay, Julio Sasaki, and Evelyn Shu came to America to study. They were determined to complete their goals because of their potential for fulfilling careers.

Make an effort to mingle with Americans

Georg Hirsch, a freelance correspondent, said, "I have seen foreigners—both Germans and other nationals—who prefer to hang out with people from their own country. It is understandable for those who are homesick and for those who are in America only temporarily. However, if you are planning to make America your home, it can hamper the process of integration. I mingled with Americans from day one. During my first two years in Washington, DC, I worked with Germans, so I avoided socializing with them in my spare time. I had American roommates and got involved in sports and other social activities. Now, after nine years in Washington, I am more relaxed about it, and yes, Germans may approach me after hours now!"

Network as much as possible

Networking is a good way to meet people who may be able to help you find jobs through word-of-mouth referrals or personal recommendations. You can network in several ways, such as by joining business, social, or special interest clubs like your local Chamber of Commerce or Toastmasters club.

If any of the groups you choose is tied in somehow to the business you are setting up, join it. Shake hands with these people. Find out who does what. And tell whoever you talk to about the type of work you do or are looking for. Remember that you are not just meeting people to meet people. You are trying to find good opportunities.

An effective way of networking for a job is to set a specific objective: say, meet ten new people or collect ten business cards. Make sure you also circulate your business card or résumé.

Strategies for Business Success

Business owners Louis Cheng and Dave Lang told me about some invaluable traits that helped them become successful entrepreneurs. Louis and Dave learned as much as they could about their businesses before starting. Thorough research and advice from friends who already owned businesses gave them insights on how to proceed. Louis' and Dave's approaches ultimately paid off, as their businesses continue to grow and succeed.

Put your customers first

Put your customers first. You always have to put yourself in their shoes. If you want the best for yourself, you should think that your customers want the best for themselves, too. If you want to retain your customers, make sure that you keep them satisfied. If they are satisfied, it could mean repeat business and recommendations to others. "When you have invested a lot of money to start a business," Cheng explained, "you cannot afford to be sloppy. You should ensure that revenue grows and loan payments are timely. If you have a business partner, it is all the more reason to do your best because failure affects both of you in many ways."

Hire the right people

It is difficult to hire people with the right mix of qualifications and interpersonal skills. I gave a "what if" scenario to a former manager. If two people vie for the same job but one is more qualified than the other but has a terrible attitude, which would you hire? She told me that she would hire the person with the better attitude who has lesser skills but who is trainable. Keep in mind that you have to work with an employee eight hours a day every day. Which of the two job applicants would you rather work with?

Treat your employees well

When you hire employees, you already know that they are qualified to do the work you hired them for. So, give them the independence without excessive supervision. Trust them. Dave Lang said, "If you treat your employees well, they will treat you the same way. When you are in a business where you have to hire the right people, you want to ensure that you keep these people. It is easier to treat them well and have them stay with you than not to treat them well and keep hiring new employees."

Dave Lang said, "Do not hire people you cannot trust. Hire only the best because it serves you well in the long run. There is high turnover especially in service businesses, and because of this, you need to be alert and keep ahead of competition. Being a good communicator helps tremendously in resolving conflicts."

7. Overcoming Obstacles

Obstacles are a normal part of life. It helps to anticipate problems and plan, but problems, often coming by surprise, can happen anytime and anywhere. Of course, many times things are not as bad as they appear and sometimes your greatest difficulties come from expecting too much too soon. One psychologist even went so far as to define failure as being the difference between what you expect and what you get.

That is not to say that you should not have goals. In fact, one common problem is that people do not always clearly identify their goals and thus do not always recognize their successes even when they have them. Therefore, you need goals, but you also need patience and must remember that it will take time to accomplish these goals and that there will be obstacles along the way.

Obstacles come in different shapes and sizes. The most common problems immigrants face are discrimination, prejudice, injustice, and hate-motivated incidents. Some obstacles are easy to overcome while others are difficult because they are beyond most people's control.

For every obstacle, you can find a solution, but it might take time and help from people and support groups. For instance, if your obstacle is the need to speak English better, the solution might be to enroll in a course on English as a second language. If you want to learn English even more quickly, you might resort to finding a volunteer tutor who will donate some of his or her time to you. You might be surprised how many people are willing to help if you let them know they are appreciated.

Another obstacle could be difficulty in getting along with coworkers and supervisors who are not used to working with people from other cultures. This issue is being addressed by many organizations, and many companies consider it an advantage to have a diverse workforce. More and more companies have set up special diversity programs to help employers and managers understand and embrace different cultures.

Everyone interviewed for this book faced numerous obstacles while adapting to life in the United States. Through persistence and determination, through hard work and a little patience, they overcame these difficulties and ultimately succeeded.

Maria Jaramillo, a retired teacher originally from Mexico, told me of a language obstacle she later overcame. “I could not pronounce English words the way they should be pronounced,” she said. “At that time, I was still learning to understand and speak English by taking classes at my church. It was tough not being able to communicate in English, especially because of the insults hurled at me by students at the grade school I attended.”

When Maria was in high school, students were forced to speak in English. The school’s rule was that students could speak Spanish only outside the school building. If students spoke Spanish in hallways or classrooms, they were sent to the principal’s office and reprimanded. Teachers monitored the students closely to ensure that they spoke in English, and if they were caught speaking in Spanish, teachers told them, “Speak English, this is not Mexico.”

Maria eventually learned how to speak English well by speaking the language every day, even outside of the classroom. Her husband and children spoke English all the time at home and were instrumental in her overcoming this obstacle.

Georg Hirsch, a foreign correspondent from Germany, initially thought his biggest problem was not having a green card. Georg said, “I was offered several side jobs, some of them lucrative, when I was relatively new to the country, but I couldn’t take them, since I only had the J-1 visa obtained for my contract with Voice of America.” Now, he thinks, his biggest obstacle is *having* a green card, with so many employment options to choose from.

Understanding Diversity

What is diversity? Diversity is a characteristic of a group or society that is made up of many kinds of people. Diversity is “otherness,” or those human qualities that are different from your own and outside the groups to which you belong. Diversity is divided into two dimensions. Primary dimensions include age, ethnicity, gender, physical abilities/qualities, race, and sexual orientation. Secondary dimensions of diversity are those that can be changed, and include, but are not limited to, educational background, geographic location, income, marital status, military experience, religious beliefs, political outlook, philosophy of life, and work experiences.

Diversity is an advantage in today's environment, and being unique actually could be in your favor. Many large organizations embrace diversity and welcome the differences. In the workplace, a diverse group of employees is an advantage. You learn from them; they learn from you. Many large organizations offer diversity programs to employees at all levels, including top management, because more and more immigrant workers enter the United States every day. (Additional information about diversity programs is available in Appendix A, *Support Groups and Multicultural Resources*.)

Stereotyping

What is a stereotype? It is an oversimplified generalization about an entire group of people without regard for individual differences. Even positive stereotypes, such as "Asians are good at math and computers," can have a negative impact when used to justify passing over an Asian-American for a job in a nontechnical field.

Stereotyping usually exaggerates a group tendency and is usually negative or has negative connotations. Stereotypes are popularly held beliefs often perpetuated by the media and unchallenged in the minds of people who have not had sufficient personal experience to counteract such beliefs. Stereotypes serve a function, often subconscious. If people can put a label on someone, they may feel justified in practicing certain behaviors.

It is important to understand the differences between an American culture and the cultures of other countries. People resort to stereotyping or labeling certain cultures based on limited perceptions—such as thinking of Asians as good *only* in technical areas or African-Americans as being good *only* in sports. Is this thinking the result of one's values, heritage, or of limited perceptions? Stereotypical perceptions of some groups may, in fact, produce a positive effect. However, in most cases, the effect on the individuals who are labeled is negative.

According to many experts, some stereotyping is unavoidable. That is because stereotyping is a basic way of absorbing information. People make connections about other people based on their observations and experience or on what they have been taught. However, such generalizations are not necessarily based on fact.

Stereotyping occurs when people make these associations all the time, experts say. "Commonly held stereotypes about Hispanics often focus on language (they speak only Spanish), families (they have a lot of children), and nationality (they are foreign-born)."

Anthony Hall, an African-American lawyer, stated, "I don't know of any group that has more stereotypes about it than African-Americans. A stereotype with a long shelf life labels blacks as having low intelligence." One that irks Hall is that blacks cannot afford to buy anything unless it is on the layaway plan. Hall also said, "Blacks, in turn, have portrayed Asians and Jews as money-grabbing exploiters of blacks." Stereotypes are fluid, changing with the times and each new group. Most immigrants to this country have suffered stereotyping, including Germans, Irish, Italians, Jews, Puerto Ricans, Gypsies, and Chinese. But some of these stereotypes, particularly those about white ethnic groups, have diminished. David Pemberton, a historian with the U.S. Census Bureau, said, "I have the feeling that stereotypes soften and may go out as ripples in a pond."

"Stereotyping among minorities" is just beginning to receive attention, said Margaret Bull Kovera, a professor at Florida International University in Miami. She said, "This is an important time to be learning more about the issue.

Benedict B. Yim, a lawyer who represents Korean business groups, says that Korean-Americans are "falsely portrayed as exploiters of the black community." Yim says, "Korean-Americans did not go to South Central Los Angeles to exploit black people. They went there because it was the cheapest area where they could afford to set up a business. Furthermore, they risked their life's savings and their lives and worked long hours providing goods and services that no one else was providing to many of these high-crime, inner-city neighborhoods."

Discrimination

What is discrimination? Discrimination is the behavior that can follow prejudicial thinking. Discrimination is the denial of justice and fair treatment in many arenas, including employment, housing, and political rights.

Even today, many immigrants feel subtle discrimination everywhere—at work, in public, at church, and elsewhere. Most try to ignore it. If they feel they are discriminated against, they often choose not to analyze what is happening. Immigrants can avoid a lot of discrimination by seeking employment in socially responsible companies that support diversity. In their attempt to attract and retain a balanced workforce, socially responsible companies often advertise that they are equal opportunity employers.

Discrimination can come from other minorities. In parts of South Florida, for example, tensions often run high between blacks and Cubans whom blacks accuse of discriminating against them. Another example is the case of minority-on-minority bias that occurred during the 1992 Rodney King riots in Los Angeles, when some blacks, reacting to a history of white police violence, singled out Korean stores to vandalize and loot.

Tips on handling discrimination

Discrimination exists under a variety of circumstances. Society in general sometimes discriminates against people for different reasons, whether in employment, housing, political affiliation, religion, race—or other situations. Yet, in many instances people who look different and speak with an accent are targets for discrimination, although it is often subtle. Because of antidiscrimination laws, larger companies especially make a conscious effort to ensure they provide equal opportunities for all employees, support a balanced workforce, and provide diversity or cross-cultural programs. Individuals often cannot stop discrimination against themselves, but they can alleviate many uncomfortable situations by reacting properly. Table 4 provides general guidelines for handling discrimination.

Table 4 - Tips on Handling Discrimination

What	How
Identify the problem	If you feel you are being discriminated against, there is a good chance you are
Confront the offender	On-the-spot is effective, but tricky. If you feel too uncomfortable, write a letter
If the situation warrants	File a formal complaint, reporting the offender and any higher-ups who may be involved
If the offender is a business	Contact your local Better Business Bureau and file a complaint
In other situations	The ACLU is a good resource for formal complaints
Help quash discrimination	Get the word out about your experience

Source: *http://racerelations.about.com.*

The Glass Ceiling

The "glass ceiling" refers to barriers to one's ability to rise within a corporate structure, which are not readily apparent or formally stated, but which are real nonetheless. The glass ceiling is named such because you can see people above you (through the "glass"), but you cannot get through yourself. The glass ceiling also applies to minority groups who are kept from advancing higher because of their race, language, gender, nationality, or other reasons.

The glass ceiling affects both men and women, especially minorities. Several people I interviewed said that a glass ceiling definitely exists at different levels in different companies, but it is so subtle that they have not noticed it much from where they are sitting. Perhaps only the people immediately below top executive levels would feel and see that the "glass ceiling" exists.

Elena Minnitti said, "A glass ceiling is an invisible barrier that prevents you from moving up. It is usually based on discrimination by gender or race. Examples are when a man and a woman are holding the exact same jobs, but the man gets paid more; or when someone gets bypassed for a promotion because of gender or race."

Julio Sasaki said, "A glass ceiling is when you get bypassed for a job that you are totally qualified for because of political factors beyond your control." Does it exist? Julio added, "Things are changing but not consistently across societies and companies. Diversity is playing a role now. There are concerns to be more diverse, which I doubt is practiced consistently across companies."

Bharat Sahay said, "I believe that there are glass ceilings at different levels and these could be between genders, race, and sometimes language. If you are considered for a top job, it is expected that you can communicate and articulate your ideas clearly to top management."

One of the most commonly asked questions about the glass ceiling is, why does it still exist? One of the most basic answers to this question is because we have not seen it clearly for what it is. Describing it more accurately becomes, potentially, a very useful activity. Talking about the glass ceiling in terms of global, societal, or philosophical issues is no substitute for defining the problem in functional terms. The more we describe the glass ceiling as the simple, tactical mechanism that continually perpetuates its existence, the clearer the means become for dismantling it.

The glass ceiling exists at multiple levels.[9]

Apprenticeship

The glass ceiling at the level of apprenticeship exists although the immediate economic consequences are not attention-getting, because very few in this category sue. Every industry has its own version of apprenticeship. In the United States, in contrast to Europe and Asia, apprenticeship is frequently completed in graduate school. For instance, a recently graduated MBA in the United States is paid a professional-level salary and is expected to make a professional-level contribution in his or her job. The same is true for a recently graduated engineer in any number of disciplines. In other arenas, such as medicine, an apprenticeship is in the form of internship or residency before full status as a doctor is granted.

In management positions, a simple way to determine the boundary of apprenticeship is to find out from your manager what line must be crossed before a person is "in the pack" to be considered for a management or leadership position. Each department in a large company has succession planning programs that list high potential employees who are identified as promotable to management positions. Salary and title may or may not change dramatically across this boundary.

The Pipeline

This is the second level of the glass ceiling. The Pipeline is the range of jobs that are post-apprenticeship, but prior to senior or top management. In nonprofit or public sector organizations, top management is best defined as people reporting directly to the executive director. Cabinet members reporting to the president of the United States would be the equivalent of top management in the public sector.

The glass ceiling can apply to all workers, both men and women, who have reached the Pipeline level. Because of this, it is easy to question whether the glass ceiling really exists. One way to see that it exists is by looking at information from the Bureau of Labor Statistics, which reveals that the ratio of men to women in all managerial positions is 1.4 to 1. Examples of the glass ceiling at this level are the pay gap and the exclusion of certain workers from credential-building experiences, as well as the discounting of the credentials that a worker does hold.

Alice in Wonderland

The third level at which the glass ceiling exists is called this because the rules and relationships seem so dramatically different for women than for men to reach top-level management positions. Although the rules and relationships apply to both men and women, it is the women who frequently feel as if they have to run as fast as they can just to stay in place; and for many, the final outcome seems to be the corporate version of "off with their heads!"

In the August 1999 issue of the *Rochester Democrat and Chronicle*,[10] Anne Mulcahy, president and chief operating officer of Xerox Corporation, wrote, "If the glass ceiling is broken, why was it such big news when a woman got the top spot at Hewlett-Packard (HP) recently? At 44, Carly Fiorina broke new ground as the first female CEO at HP. But she did not break the glass ceiling that continues to be a barrier for most women in technology. This is not to underestimate the significance of Fiorina's appointment. It is a momentous accomplishment. Companies like HP do not gamble with CEOs. As an outsider with a proven track record, Fiorina was viewed as the finest candidate for the job. The fact that she happens to be a woman is incidental."

In another case, a minority woman, Andrea Jung, was appointed CEO for Avon Products, the largest U.S. company to be run by an Asian-American woman. Jung started as an Avon consultant in 1993 and became president and CEO in 1998. Pretty impressive.

Pressures that women face in breaking the glass ceiling

The glass ceiling exists, though it may be subtle. To break it, you must prepare yourself well if you aspire to be in a management position. It is still not an easy road, especially for women executives. A few have broken the ceiling, such as Andrea Jung. It is not impossible, but it is not easy either. Following are common obstacles for women in the workplace.

The job itself

The demands of a top-level executive job are often unrelenting, hectic, and involve long hours. The responsibilities are enormous. The job also involves socializing with other executives such as playing golf, going out for drinks after work, and other social activities. If you are a woman with a family, you might find it difficult to balance your work and family life well.

Being a woman is a pressure in itself

The pressure created by having to set an example for all women, or as it is commonly said, as a "role model" and a "first" along with personal competency, is tremendous. You have to deal with added pressures that men do not have to deal with.

Managing the demands in life outside of work

If you are married with children, you are still expected to take major responsibilities for maintaining a household, raising children, and even nurturing an intimate relationship. It would help if you have an understanding spouse who can share family responsibilities. But balancing work and family even with help is not easy. If you are a single woman, you may not find a personal life outside of work.

Advice for executives

Any successful executive needs at least a few of the following critical success factors:

A track record of achievements

Help from above is only one factor; you still need certain abilities to complement that help and justify it. Having a proven record means always excelling in your work assignments through technical competence, professionalism, and the ability to anticipate and solve problems, leadership skills, or anything else your job requires, such as adding to the company's bottom line.

Desire to succeed

As an executive, you survive by having a burning desire to be successful. You can show it by demonstrating your personal drive, working hard, seizing more responsibilities, and pushing things to the limit until you have completed your job. Remember that by doing all these you have to pay the price. Work comes first, which is especially difficult if you have to sacrifice by working long hours and putting your family life on the "back burner." Being single has its advantages because you do not have to balance family and work, although your social life may be nonexistent.

Ability to manage subordinates

Complementary to having a proven track record, you need the ability to hire the right people and improve the performance of your employees. Excellent communication and interpersonal skills are good formulas for success. You can acquire the skill of managing subordinates by attending training on the subject and learning on the job through the help of a mentor who can provide coaching.

Willingness to take career risks

This could mean changing jobs, accepting high-risk assignments, moving from staff to line jobs, demanding a promotion, or in some cases, being your own boss by starting your own business.

Ability to be tough, decisive, and demanding

With so many expectations, who said that being an executive is easy? Acting hard-nosed and not tentative in making decisions are tough approaches, but these behaviors are connected to how well you perform in an executive role.

Ability to think on your feet

As an executive, you are faced with situations in which you have to respond to questions or issues on the spot. Pausing for a moment and collecting your thoughts will help you provide well-thought-out responses.

Good analytical skills

Most executive jobs require good analytical skills, but as a manager, you have to be able to synthesize, analyze, interpret, and report financial results. Even if you have financial controllers who support you, you are still ultimately accountable for ensuring that your organization is financially stable.

A positive image

Being able to think on your feet and have good analytical skills is not enough. You have to present yourself well and possess all other personal skills, self-confidence, and business savvy expected of executives. It is important in this competitive world that you have what it takes. Communicating clearly with your peers as well as with people who look up to you is critical.

Willingness to push for success

All the success factors I described have to do with getting along and getting things done smoothly, working through others, adapting, and being easy to be with. The ability to work with others—subordinates, managers, and peers—is a strength.

Ability to maintain good relationships

One reason many people call "networking" important is that it enables you to handle matrix relationships, maintaining key relations with your customers, focusing in on power people, and knowing whom to call for what and when. Of course, political, interpersonal, and leadership skills are of utmost importance.

Help from above

It is not easy to survive in top-level management positions if you do not have a mentor who is also at the top. You need both detailed advice and general encouragement in addition to highly visible assignments. You also may need help from those higher than your immediate boss, even those at the very top of the corporation.

Breaking through the glass ceiling

As an executive, you carry a heavy load of responsibilities, but you pay a high price to get a chance at a top job. Following are several ways you can break through:

Credibility

You must prove that you are top management material before you can earn the necessary promotions, and you need to constantly perform in an outstanding manner. At the Pipeline level, you should not allow others to take credit for work you have done. Rather, you should be assertive about making your accomplishments known.

Advocacy

You need help from top management to get the kind of experience required to be promoted. Having a strong advocate or support system plays a major role in your ability to move up. You cannot do it alone. You need a senior manager on your side—for example, a mentor who is in top management. What you have to do is to recruit your own mentor in order to have access to important credential-building experiences. You will want your mentor also to be good with people, influential, and politically savvy. These qualities would suggest that your mentor/advocate is competent himself or herself and well-regarded in the company.

Outright luck

You need a break or two. This could happen in different ways, such as your meeting someone who is hiring people in your field of expertise. Success might come with getting into a business that is on the upswing, or playing a role in a project that attracts national attention. Being in the right place at the right time is not enough. Luck and ability are often related. Examples of how luck can join with ability to help you succeed include having a boss who is willing to promote and push you for a management position, or being the only woman around at the time who knows something about a problem.

Racism

The effects of racism can be devastating. Racism is a prejudice and/or discrimination based on myths of race. Racists believe that some groups are born superior to others, and in the name of protecting their race from "contamination," they justify the domination and destruction of races they consider to be inferior to their own. If you are a victim, you can be physically and emotionally harmed or your property can be damaged or destroyed.

Hate crimes are violent acts against people, property, or organizations because of the group to which you belong or identify with. This type of crime is a tragic part of American history. However, it was not until early in the 1990s that the federal government began to collect data on how many and what kind of hate crimes are being committed, and by whom.

Many hate crimes are committed by law-abiding young people who see little wrong with their actions. Alcohol and drugs sometimes help fuel these crimes, but the main determinant appears to be personal prejudice, a situation that colors people's judgment, blinding the aggressors to the immorality of what they are doing. Such prejudice most likely is rooted in an environment that encourages hating a group of people who are perceived to be "different" or inferior, and views an individual's perceived difference as representative of what is most threatening about the group as a whole.

Racial violence

Hate crimes are often linked with racial violence because the motivation for hate is based on hostility toward people of a different race, skin color, religion, ancestry, or national origin. However, hate crimes also victimize those whose differences comprise sexual orientation and gender. Racial violence can happen anywhere—where you live, go to school, or work. Wherever it occurs, racial violence affects the peace and security of the entire community.

Racial violence can be either subtle or extreme. Some examples of the different forms of racial violence include:

- Intimidation: physical and verbal threats, hateful glares.
- Harassment: insults, shoving, or racist hate propaganda.
- Physical violence: assault with or without a weapon.

Typical hate crime laws criminalize the use of force, or the threat of force, against a person who is perceived to be a member of a

Table 5 - Steps for Handling Racial Harassment

Situation	Solution
If you feel threatened or in danger	Dial 911 for help. 911 is a telephone help service available 24 hours a day to anyone in an emergency situation. The operator will immediately contact the police or other emergency service. For communities without a 911 service, contact the emergency number listed on the inside of the telephone directory, or dial 0 for the operator.
Record the details of the incident	Try to record as much information as you can. Useful information includes: • Date, time, and place of the incident(s) • The circumstances of the incident • Description of the attacker(s), including details such as height, hair, eye color and clothing • Description of any cars, including make, model, year, license plate, color • Name, telephone number and address of witnesses (if any) • Name and badge number of the assisting police officers and district where they work • Medical report of any injury • Photographs and insurance reports of any property damage
If you deal with the police	• Have someone with you for support and reassurance (you may, for example, wish to have a neighbor, a friend, or passer-by with you) • Ask for a translator if you do not speak or understand English • Ask about police procedures in dealing with racial violence • Do not forget to ask for the file number of the case • Ask the police to follow up your complaint and inform you of its status
If you are victimized by hate groups	Call one of the organizations listed at your local County Community Service Guide

Source: http://racerelations.about.com

specific, protected group. Ironically, many hate crimes seem random and not predictable by the type of neighborhood.

The word "perceived" is important, because many vicious assaults are based on the incorrect belief that the victim is Jewish, gay, or a member of some other group that the perpetrator hates. Thus, if a thug beats up a victim he randomly selected because of his or her race, that is a hate crime.

In the May 18, 2000, issue of the *Los Angeles Times*,[11] an article discussed Joseph Ileto, a Filipino-American, who was allegedly slain by a white supremacist. Joseph was senselessly killed because he was perceived to be black.

Hate crimes have become increasingly common on college campuses in the United States. For example, in 1999 at Dartmouth College, anti-Semitic statements were reported in the school newspaper. It was no different at the University of Wisconsin when an unknown hatemonger spray-painted "Think Extinction" on the walls of the Jewish Student Center.

8. Finding Help

New arrivals to America who do not have family or friends to support them may need additional help, especially during the first few months when they are still getting settled. Often, the first point of contact is their church, although there are many other resources for help, such as community associations and government agencies that offer free services.

Many of the people I interviewed overcame the difficulties of adjustment with the passage of time and experience. Support from others was especially important to those who came to America when they were young and single. Most found help from friends and relatives, local churches and their communities. Those who were more independent often did well on their own, relying more on patience, determination, and ambition than on support groups.

After they arrived from Vietnam, Dave Lang and his family were fortunate to be sponsored by a family from Kansas, who provided his family food and housing for a full year. The people at his Lutheran church helped him and his family by donating clothes, kitchen utensils, and household supplies.

Support Groups

Support groups provide a variety of help ranging from social and emotional issues to legal and financial issues. The government often provides funding and many of the services are free. Other support groups are privately funded and may also offer free services. You can find a list of support groups at the library or on the Web. You will also find that community groups and churches can be of help. Many support groups can help you with financial, legal, and immigration issues.

Churches

When Nora Szeto arrived in America, her only support group (other than her sister and a close friend) was her church, where she found solace and comfort, especially during Sunday masses when she sings in the choir. Most of her interactions are with other choir singers—fellow immigrants and native-born Americans.

You can find churches through the yellow pages of the telephone directory or by asking friends, relatives, and neighbors. You may even find your church by driving around. Resources will vary depending on your religion. You will find that in every community, there are houses of worship that cater to different ethnic groups. It should not be difficult to find a church that suits your needs.

Associations

Associations are organizations of people having common interests, purposes, and ideas. Associations are funded either by the government or by nonprofit private organizations. Many associations in the United States help common people resolve economic, social, legal, and immigration problems. Following are examples of several associations:

Center for Education, Employment and Community (CEEC)
The Center for Education, Employment and Community works for the economic and social well-being of all. This association brings together people of diverse talents and backgrounds to create systems that help students learn new skills, workers advance in their careers, and citizens improve their communities.

CEEC is part of Education Development Center, Inc. (EDC). EDC is committed to education that builds knowledge and skills, makes possible a deeper understanding of the world, and engages learners as active, problem-solving participants.

American Immigration Network (AIN)
The American Immigration Network offers a wide variety of services, including U.S. immigration assistance for individuals and businesses by a team of experienced, licensed immigration lawyers. This group also recommends the Do-it-Yourself U.S. immigration kits as an inexpensive alternative to retaining an attorney. Visit the AIN Web site at *www.usavisanow.com* for additional information.

National Neighborhood Coalition (NNC)
The National Neighborhood Coalition serves as a crucial link to Washington for neighborhood and community-based organizations and an important networking resource for representatives of regional and national organizations involved in community development, housing, and a wide range of other neighborhood issues. Readers

benefit from NNC by joining their worthwhile initiatives, one of which is the Family-to-Family Initiative. Visit the Web site *www.neighborhoodcoalition.org.*

You can also find other national neighborhood coalitions from a nonprofit organization. An example is the Study Circles Resource Center (SCRC). SCRC helps communities organize study circles—small-group, democratic, peer-led discussions that give people opportunities to make a difference in their neighborhoods and communities by bringing hundreds and sometimes thousands of diverse people into dialogue and action on critical issues facing their communities, such as building strong neighborhoods; growth and sprawl; racism and race relations; crime and violence; education reform; diversity; immigration; and criminal justice. SCRC is one of the initiatives of NNC, so you can access information about it from Web site *www.neighborhoodcoalition.org.*

Self-Help

Many of those interviewed felt that, in addition to taking advantage of support groups, there are many things you can do for yourself to achieve success. Following are some examples:

Reach out to your community

You can develop your own support groups by reaching out to neighbors in the community where you live or parishioners in your church.

In many communities, neighborhood events, such as block parties, are a good way of meeting your neighbors. You bring a dish to the party and introduce yourself to others. This can benefit your children in particular if they happen to go to the same school as your neighbors' children. You may also want to have your own party and invite your neighbors to get to know them better.

If you live in a planned community, you may have amenities such as a fitness center, jogging and walking paths, and tennis courts. If you like to walk and your spouse does not, you may befriend a neighbor or someone in your community to have someone to walk with.

Join a community group

Community groups are another resource to seek help. Many communities have formed their own neighborhood coalitions. For example, the San Marcos Co-housing Association in Texas is a group of local people who are pooling their resources to create a "custom neighborhood." These are people with varied interests, beliefs, and backgrounds who want homes in harmony with their contemporary lives.

Co-housing is an idea that began in Denmark thirty years ago with some young families who wanted a better place to raise their children. They realized that a good community is where people who know and trust each other cooperate to make their lives easier and more enriched. They also understood how good neighborhood design that focused on proximity and people instead of cars can help neighbors collaborate and strengthen their sense of community.

A list of community and neighborhood groups can be found in local telephone books and county brochures. The local library and the Internet are also very good sources for finding such groups. Many new arrivals to America have joined community groups. One contributor told me, "If you are active within your community, it is much easier to ask for help. If you live in planned residential communities, participate in activities."

Join a social group or charity

People who join social or charitable groups volunteer their free time and services to help people in need. Many who are engaged in these activities are retirees who work part-time and want to get involved in more meaningful social activities where they can meet people with their same interests. For people who are in business, these groups are a good way to network and make new contacts.

Participate in school activities

Most schools offer a variety of political, social, and academic activities. You might want to run for school office or become involved in a political organization at school. Joining such a group will also expose you to opportunities once you graduate and want to become involved with local politics in your community. You can also take advantage of field trips and join fraternity or sorority groups.

Find a mentor

What is a mentor? A mentor is defined as an experienced person who provides guidance and support in a variety of ways to the developing novice by being a role model (show by example), guide, tutor, or coach. The term "mentoring" is everywhere these days—in books and in office manuals, in formal presentations and casual conversation, and in companies that have mentoring programs. If the definition of "mentor" leaves considerable room for interpretation, so does the practice of mentoring. What does a mentor do, and how, and how much? All these depend on the individual mentor.

In schools, mentoring is just as important in any profession. Most schools have job placement centers, which is a good starting place to look for a counselor (a person who gives advice or general career guidance). Mentors—either an experienced and trusted counselor or teacher—play a crucial role in ensuring that a student gets valuable advice.

Additional resources for obtaining help can be found in Appendix A, *Support Groups and Multicultural Resources.*

Part III

Visiting the United States the First Time

9. Obtaining a Visa

Each year millions of people from dozens of countries apply for U.S. visas. Preparation often takes more time than the processing itself.

Obtaining a visa involves different processes depending on the type of visa you are applying for. People who come on immigrant visas usually start the process years before they get approval to come to America. The process is usually much faster for non-immigrant visas, but the length of time can vary greatly depending on the type of visa.

The fastest process, based on my experience, is getting a tourist visa. As soon as your passport and supporting documents (bank accounts, affidavits of support) are ready, you can call the U.S. Embassy in your country to schedule an interview with a consular officer. Your travel agent can do all the processing for you and can also help arrange the interview. After the interview with a consular officer, you will know immediately if your visa is approved or not.

Depending on the type of visa you are applying for, the documents required may differ. Students need an acceptance letter from an American school, while tourists must present the necessary financial statements to assure the U.S. Embassy that they can afford to visit America.

There are many types of visas, although each falls under one of two broad categories—immigrant and non-immigrant. (See Tables 6 and 7 for the classification types of non-immigrant and immigrant visas.)

The immigrants I interviewed (permanent residents or green card holders) had an easier adjustment than the non-immigrants (tourists, students, or contract people). They did not have to worry about employment because they were legally allowed to work anywhere in America. After all, they went through proper channels to get their visas. They said, "We waited patiently for our papers and paid our dues, so we are free to work and live anywhere we wish."

On the other hand, the non-immigrants I interviewed (tourists, students, and those with work permits) had many and varied immigration issues to contend with. The tourists could only stay in America for several months to a year, while the students could stay only until they completed their studies. The students had an edge over the tourists since they were able to work, although their terms of employment limited them to school-related work on and off campus. Those with work permits were also limited to working within the conditions specified in their work contracts.

Non-Immigrant Visas

Non-immigrants coming to the United States from most countries are required to obtain a visa. Whether the visa is for business, tourism, or other purposes, it will expire at a predesignated date. Unless the visa is renewed, the holder must leave the United States.

Student visas

Student visas are issued to students for the duration of studies up to eight years. F-1 visas are issued to full-time academic or language students, while M-1 visas are issued to vocational and other non-academic students. M-1 visa holders are admitted for the time necessary to complete their courses plus 30 days, or for one year, whichever is less. Extensions may be requested. F-1 and M-1 visas have the same prerequisites and limitations, although they differ slightly in the application procedure and the form used.

If you come to the United States on an F-1 visa, you must be enrolled in a program leading to a degree or certificate. An F-1 visa is normally obtained when you are in your home country and have selected a specific school to enroll in. A visa can be issued quickly, especially if you have already received an acceptance from the school. Transfer from one school to another or from one program to another is allowed via a simple procedure, which is to notify the Immigration and Naturalization Service (INS) of the change.

Table 6 - Non-Immigrant Visas

Classification type	Description
A-1. Foreign government official A-2. Employees A-3. Family and servants	Diplomatic—foreign government official or employee, family, and servants.
B-1. Temporary visitor for business	Usually for short-term business trips but can be for up to a one-year stay initially, renewable at six-month periods thereafter.
B-2. Temporary visitor for pleasure	Cannot work in United States. Valid for six months' stay, extensions allowed.
E-1. Treaty trader E-2. Treaty investor	For extended stay for business personnel overseeing or working for an enterprise in the United States that is engaged in trade between the United States and a treaty country, or that represents a major investment in the United States.
F-1. Student	Issued to students who applied for visas from own country. Visa is valid for the duration of studies (up to eight years).
H-1B. Temporary professional worker	For people who are coming to perform professional services in a specialty profession; e.g., specialty occupations.
J-1. Exchange visitor or student	Students admitted for duration of studies plus 18 months for practical training; business and industrial trainees are admitted for 18 months; teachers and scholars have a three-year limit; professors and researchers may stay for longer periods; extensions can be obtained.
M-1. Vocational and other nonacademic student	Admitted for time necessary to complete course plus 30 days, or for one year—whichever is less; extensions may be sought.

Source: *Immigrating to the USA*, Dan P. Danilov, Bellingham, WA: Self-Counsel Press Legal Series, 1999.[12]

If you are on a scholarship or fellowship, you are allowed to work part-time on campus. You can also work off-campus upon receiving special permission from the school, as long as the job provides training related to your field of study. As a student, you are allowed to travel in and out of the United States or remain in the United States until the completion of your studies—up to the maximum of eight years. This time period is useful since many students come to the United States to pursue doctoral degrees, which take seven to eight years to complete.

Elena Minnitti came on an F-1 visa. While enrolled as a scholar at the State University of New York, she worked as a teaching and research assistant. The school gave her a stipend (allowance) and paid for her tuition. A number of her classmates came with J-1 visas, which are for exchange students or scholars. They received scholarships from their governments or from U.S. agencies. However, those who came with J-1 visas were required to return to their countries of origin immediately after graduation. They were not allowed to return to the United States until they had spent two years in their own countries.

The students I interviewed said that the processing of their student visas was cumbersome. They had to complete many forms both for the schools they applied for in America, and for the U.S. Embassy in their home countries. However, the foreign students told me, "Once you get acceptance from the school of your choice and get an approved student visa from the U.S. consulate, waiting to leave for America is something you look forward to with great anticipation and excitement."

Temporary workers

Temporary workers may qualify for several types of visas. The most common is the H-1B professional category. For H-1B visas, American companies petition the government for the visa beneficiary, and the position must be professional in nature, such as engineering, medicine and health, or architecture.

Other types of temporary working visas include TN-1 (Free Trade Professional), E-2 (Investor–Long-lasting U.S. Visa for Canadian Investors), and L-1 (Canadian company related to a U.S. company). For each of the temporary working visas, the duration of stay in the United States may vary. For example, if you are on an L-1 visa status, the total time limit on this category is seven years stay for executives/managers; five for others.

Since Elena Minnitti was already in the country on an F-1 visa, she was allowed to keep her visa for one year after graduation so she could work and get practical training in her field of chemistry. Elena had to obtain a temporary professional worker visa (H-1B) in order to continue working in the United States. Because of her doctoral degree and extensive experience in chemistry, she was fortunate to get the visa through company sponsorship.

However, many people who come on H-1B visas are recruited directly from their home countries. Elena said that she knows a number of people with "hot" technical skills (in computers, the sciences, nursing, etc.) who were able to get employment through H-1B visas. They sent job applications directly to U.S. companies that hire foreign nationals due to the shortage of skilled workers in their industries. After these people arrived in the United States, and after proving themselves to be good workers, it was much easier for them to obtain sponsorship for a green card.

Exchange visitors

Exchange visitors hold J-1 visas. Gabrielle Wittner came from Switzerland as an exchange visitor via an au pair trial program, while Georg Hirsch came from Germany as an exchange visitor to work for the Voice of America as a correspondent.

Gabrielle came to the United States through the help of a special agency. The sponsor of the exchange visitor program provided a J-1 visa form that listed the specific dates that she was expected to participate in the program. Gabrielle was authorized to remain in the United States only up to one year, as indicated on the Certificate of Eligibility. The Certificate of Eligibility is usually issued for the period of time needed to complete the exchange visitor program. INS regulations, however, place some maximum time limits on J-1 visas according to the type of program.

Gabrielle applied for the au pair trial program while she was still in her home country of Switzerland. Once she was approved, the agency found a suitable family for her in the United States. The process continued when the interested family interviewed Gabrielle by telephone and she, in turn, sent them her picture—a practice requested by many families.

In the au pair trial program, the family asks the processing agency about the background of the au pair who will be assigned to work in their household. Just as in hiring a live-in baby-sitter or housekeeper in America, families want to ensure that they hire someone who is emotionally stable, has experience taking care of small children, and is responsible enough to do household chores when mom and dad are away at work.

Not everything falls into place smoothly the first time. It sometimes happens that the family and the au pair are incompatible. Gabrielle explained to me that if you are not compatible with the first family that accepts you, you can discuss your problem with the au pair agency, and they can help find another suitable family for you to work for. But you can make only one change. If you are already on your second family, you have to make the relationship work. There is no going back, because the au pair has signed a one-year contract.

Gabrielle said, "I work for an American family and get paid for a ten-hour, five-day-a-week job primarily taking care of three school-aged children and doing laundry. I have a bedroom, a bathroom, and use of two cars. I use one car to drive and pick up the kids to and from their schools. I use the other car for my personal use, when I go out during my free time. I go out with my friends, mostly other au pairs. Although I get paid for what I do, I am frustrated that I cannot go to nightclubs because in America you have to be twenty-one to drink liquor. In Switzerland, you are able to order liquor at age eighteen. The family I live with does not cook homemade meals. They do not even have pots and pans. Every day, we are on the same diet of frozen dinners or microwaveable meals."

If the au pair (nanny) program interests foreign nationals, they should check with the U.S. Information Agency from their home countries for the names of approved au pair agencies and see if this option is still available.

Au pairs are not the only ones who fall into the J-1 category; others include technical experts, foreign students, industrial and business trainees, medical interns and residents, scholars, and foreign government employees. Sponsors may include recognized international agencies and organizations having U.S. memberships and offices.

Georg Hirsch said that he was given a J-1 visa when he worked for the Voice of America from 1991 through 1993. He added, "The big issue about the J-1 visa is that you have to go back to your home country for two years before you can apply for a green card. For some J-1 visa holders, this can be a serious obstacle. The idea behind the two-year stay-home rule is that foreigners who were supported by the American government should share with their own people the knowledge they gained in America before establishing themselves in the United States. To get around this two-year stay-home rule and be eligible to apply for a green card right away, you need a waiver from the INS."

Georg got the waiver because he convinced the INS that he was in a much better position to share knowledge of America with Germans if he could stay in America working as a foreign correspondent for the German media. He said, "The situation may be different for, say, a young doctor from Africa who works for the National Institute of Health (NIH) on a J-1 visa where he or she learns how to fight the Ebola virus. When the doctor's two-year assignment is completed, he or she might want to stay in America instead of going home to Africa. But America's response is that a doctor should go back to Africa and help fight the Ebola virus. Once America believes that a doctor who is applying for permanent residency has 'saved enough' people in his or her country, he or she can come back to America."

Tourists/temporary visitors

Tourists/visitors visas are temporary visas for business (B-1) and for pleasure (B-2). If you enter the United States with a B visa, the law requires that your intention is just to visit temporarily and then return to your home country.

A B-1 visa allows you to remain in the United States for business purposes; however, you may not be employed, set up your own company, or be paid by a source inside the United States. On a B-1 visa, it is sometimes difficult to draw the line between what is permissible business activity and what is illegal employment, but generally your agenda must be limited to making investments, buying goods, attending seminars, or performing temporary work for an employer located outside the United States.

A B-2 visa allows you to be in the United States for pleasure, which means you cannot work in the United States. Your visa is valid for six months' stay—with extensions. This means that after six months, you must leave the country or apply for an extension to stay for another six months by going to the INS in your local jurisdiction. Extensions are not automatic; INS reviews applications on a case-by-case basis.

Tourists who overstay their visas will surely not have a comfortable standing with the INS. If they overstay, there is a strong likelihood that their names will appear in immigration docket controls where they can be picked up for possible deportation. If someone tips off INS or someone reports that tourists are working illegally, in sweatshops, for instance, they will certainly be investigated, if not immediately processed for deportation. These tip-offs are not unheard of. And any person who reports a tourist working illegally will get paid a monetary reward; the amount of the reward for turning in an illegal alien varies from state to state.

Lina Shoobridge came to America on a tourist visa. Once she arrived in America, she looked for diplomatic jobs where she could get her visa converted to an international visa. Her visa was converted from a B-2 to a G-4 by virtue of her working for the World Bank. After she got married the first time and went back to England, she worked for the International Finance Corporation in London. Working there helped her return to America easily the second time. Since 1993, she has been working for the International Monetary Fund, again on a G-4 visa.

Immigrant Visas

An immigrant (also called a "lawful permanent resident or a green card holder") is a foreign national who has been granted the privilege of permanently living and working in the United States. Immigrant visas fall into employment or family categories. Table 7 lists the most common types of immigrant visas.

Several of the people I interviewed came as immigrants under employment-based or family-based preferences. Only one came seeking asylum. By virtue of being permanent residents of the United States, they were allowed to work in the United States without problems.

Table 7 - Immigrant Visas

Classification type	Description
Group 1 - Employment	
Employment Based 1st Preference	Priority workers, people of extraordinary ability, outstanding professors and researchers, and multinational managers and executives.
Employment Based 2nd Preference	Members of the professions holding advanced degrees or persons of exceptional ability (includes national interest waiver).
Employment Based 3rd Preference	Skilled workers, professionals, and other workers.
Employment Based 4th Preference	Certain special immigrants.
Employment Based 5th Preference	Employment creation investors.
Group 2 - Family	
1st Preference	Unmarried sons and daughters of U.S. citizens.
2nd Preference - A	Spouses, and children unmarried and under age 21, of permanent residents.
2nd Preference - B	Unmarried sons and daughters, age 21 or older, of permanent residents.
3rd Preference	Married sons and daughters of U.S. citizens, said citizens age 21 or older.
4th Preference	Brothers and sisters of U.S. citizens, and citizens age 21 or older.

Sources: Web sites *www.foreignborn.com* and *www.grasmick.com.*[13]

Refugees/asylees

Refugees are those who are unwilling to, or cannot, return to their country of origin because they fear persecution based on several factors: race, religion, nationality, political views, or tyranny. Each year, the president of the United States, together with Congress, decides on the number of applicants who will be admitted to the United States as refugees or asylees. The refugee application processes are complex and are handled on a case-by-case basis.

Dave Lang and his family came to America as refugees during the fall of Saigon. He said, "Processing paperwork and waiting at refugee camps until a family sponsors you can be nerve-wracking. We were fortunate to get sponsored by one family quickly. Our sponsors provided food and housing, and charitable organizations provided clothes and other basic necessities. Our family received help for one year until my siblings and I found gainful employment at restaurants, hotels, and retail stores."

Liklik Schroeder (and her siblings) came to America from the Philippines on a family-based preference. Liklik's mother sponsored the remaining unmarried siblings to join her in Livermore, California. Because they were permanent residents, all were able to work in the United States.

Green cards

Green cards are available mostly to those who have immediate family members in the United States or job skills in demand by U.S. employers. Also, a large number of green cards are given to educated professionals, investors, and refugees (people who flee for safety), or are distributed on a lottery basis (as under the Amnesty Act of 1982) to those with very few qualifications other than luck.

If you want to be employed in the United States, you need a green card. Most come to the United States with green cards already obtained from family preference sponsorships (usually, mother or father). You can also apply on your own, and you might be able to obtain a green card through an employer. To qualify, you must have a job offer from a U.S. employer, and must have the correct background in terms of education and work experience for the job.

Immigration Laws

The United States Congress enacted into law changes to immigration policies in order to handle the plight of refugees and arrival of illegal aliens, and the liberalization of trade agreements. So much has happened to the United States' relationships with other countries that in the 1990s, Presidents George Bush and Bill Clinton had to do something about continuing immigration problems.

For example, the North American Free Trade Agreement (NAFTA), which was approved by Congress in 1993, made changes to the INS regulations establishing procedures for the temporary entry of Canadian and Mexican citizen-business people into the United States. This rule facilitates the temporary entry of visitors, treaty traders, investors, temporary workers, and professionals on a reciprocal basis among the United States, Canada, and Mexico, while recognizing the continued need to ensure border security and to protect local workers and permanent employment in all three countries. Table 8 lists several key immigration laws.

Table 8 - Key Immigration Laws

Legislation	Description
Refugee Act	A system developed in 1980 to handle refugees as a class separate from other immigrants. Under the new law, refugees are defined as those who flee a country because of persecution "on account of race, religion, nationality, or political opinion."
Immigration Act of 1990 (INMAT 90)	The Act signed into law by President Bush on November 29, 1990. It represented the most extensive change in all areas of immigration in over fifty years.
North American Free Trade Agreement (NAFTA)	North American Free Trade Agreement, approved by Congress in 1993. The Agreement liberalizes trade between the United States and Canada and Mexico, and contains immigration provisions. NAFTA affects four categories of business people, equivalent to INS non-immigrant categories. There is no limit to the number of Canadians who can enter the U.S. annually but no more than 5,000 citizens of Mexico can be admitted each year.
Illegal Immigration Reform and Immigrant Responsibility Act of 1997 (IIRAIRA)	The Act signed into law by President Clinton, effective April 1, 1997. It made extensive changes to the immigration laws affecting the arrival of aliens, their treatment by the Immigration Court, and available forms of relief.

Sources: Web sites *www.grasmick.com* and *www.foreignborn.com.*[14]

Naturalization

Undoubtedly, becoming a naturalized U.S. citizen is a memorable moment. You feel elated when you hear the judge ask everyone to stand up to take the oath of allegiance. Different emotions overcome you, such as excitement and feeling of belonging. Often, the excitement is fleeting. Once you have received your citizenship and have registered to vote, people still may regard you as different because of the way you look and talk. But it does not matter. Deep in your heart, you know that you "belong."

Except in rare cases, no one can become a naturalized U.S. citizen without first having a green card. To qualify for citizenship, you must have held your green card and be physically present in the United States for a minimum of five years. If you leave the United States and remain away for a year or more, it wipes out any time toward the five-year total and you must start adding up your time from when you return.

If you are married to a U.S. citizen, you need to wait only three years to apply for U.S. citizenship. The law specifies that at least one-half of your time must have been spent physically inside U.S. boundaries. The same rules about long absences apply to those with only three-year waiting periods.

One good thing about being married to a U.S. citizen, however, is that if your American-citizen spouse is employed abroad by the U.S. government (e.g., USAID or Peace Corps), there is no waiting period and no required residency period to get U.S. citizenship. You may apply for naturalization upon receiving your green card.

As an example, Alma Barnes, who worked for the Peace Corps, married an officer of the U.S. Agency for International Development. She received her U.S. citizenship in one day since she and her husband had to leave the United States the next day for his first tour of duty.

In my case, I waited only three years because my spouse was a naturalized U.S. citizen. I was not in a hurry to change my citizenship at that time. What pushed me to apply for naturalization was double taxation. As a permanent resident from the Philippines, I had to pay taxes to my government as well as to the U.S. government. That did not bode well with me. I was frustrated that I had to pay double for one income. Being a U.S. citizen with a U.S. passport also gave me the luxury to travel to other countries without problems.

Changing Your Visa

Changing your visa from non-immigrant to immigrant status can be tricky. Approval depends on the type of visa held before a change occurs to permanent resident or green card. There are many ways to obtain a green card, although each one carries the same privileges, which include the right to work and the right to live in the United States permanently. It is not as easy or as quick as it sounds, however, and applications are processed and approved on a case-by-case basis.

For instance, I have changed my visa many times. Initially, I came on a B-2 (Tourist Visa for Pleasure), changed to A-2 (Diplomatic Visa), became a green card holder, changed to G-4 (International Visa), went back to a permanent resident visa (green card), and, finally, it was time to quit playing around and I became a naturalized U.S. citizen.

Whether you are seeking an immigrant or non-immigrant visa, you may need an immigration lawyer to help you with immigration issues or to advise you on legal matters, especially if you plan to start a business. You might want to hire an immigration lawyer who has been recommended by others. If you can afford it, you should not hesitate to hire a lawyer to process your case.

If you have trouble affording a lawyer, you can contact the American Immigration Network (AIN), whose lawyers charge a minimal fee. In many larger cities, there are support groups that can provide help with legal issues related to immigration. Additional information about these groups can be found in Appendix A, *Support Groups and Multicultural Resources*.

11. Traveling to the United States

Traveling to the United States can take months of preparation and planning. You have to abide by the rules and follow the procedures dictated by the U.S. Embassy or consulate in your home country. Processing the paperwork can be overwhelming, and completing all the requirements for a visa interview may cause anxiety. If you are coming to the United States merely for a visit, you may need only a few weeks to put it all together. Obviously, if you are coming to live in the United States permanently, it is a different situation, because of all the documentation requirements, and because you may be leaving family and friends behind.

Preparing to Emigrate

Coming to a new country is like starting a new life. It is not a matter of just picking up where you left off. You will face significant changes and differences in the beginning that you could not have imagined before your arrival in America. As noted earlier, being able to speak English well is important. If you do not speak English, consider enrolling in a class before embarking on a significant trip.

Other than being able to speak English, you need to be able to communicate your ideas clearly if you want to be gainfully employed, especially in your own profession. It is also a good idea to spend time learning about American culture before you leave your home country.

Arranging for Travel

People who plan to emigrate to America can either arrange their own travel or arrange it through a travel agency. More and more immigrants use travel agencies because the process is often cumbersome. Processing all of the paperwork without help can be difficult and time-consuming. Travel agencies can do much of this work. Their personnel know what is needed, where to go, and whom to contact. Travel agencies that arrange for international travel every day also have regular contacts at U.S. embassies. This is a big advantage since they usually know the immigration officers and are more likely to get an early interview date.

Preparation for travel to the United States can be tedious if not nerve-wracking. Arranging for your travel before you emigrate takes time. Even with help from a travel agent, you have to do some work yourself, such as researching information and putting together a travel checklist to ensure that you have everything you need before you leave. During the trip, you have to prepare for contingencies in case you get sick, have long layovers waiting for your connecting flights, or suffer delays getting through immigration and customs inspection before you reach your final destination. Once you are in the United States, you have to learn how to get around. If you are on your own without friends or family to meet you and show you around, you might find it doubly difficult, especially if you do not speak English.

Conducting research

Most people obtain information about the United States before leaving their home countries. How they get their information may differ. Some may be comfortable calling friends or relatives already in America who can easily provide information on places to see, appropriate clothes to wear, and the amount of money to bring. Many prefer calling friends or relatives in America to be assured they are getting firsthand information.

Because of advancing technology, more and more people use the Internet at their schools, in libraries, or at home to search for information about schools, jobs, and places to live. Those who do not speak English may write to the schools for brochures in their own language. Other immigrants might research topics such as American history.

Of all the immigrants who spoke with me, the students did the most formal research; others found information through family and friends.

Travel checklist

A travel checklist is useful to have. It helps you keep track of arrangements you have made and those you still need to take care of before you leave. Make several copies of the same checklist if you plan to travel again. Table 9 includes a sample checklist, which is not exhaustive but at least gives you the most important items.

Table 9 - Travel Checklist

Items	**Put a (√) when done**
Airline reservations	
Airline tickets	
Travel itinerary*	
Hotel reservations (if needed)	
Car rental (if needed)	
Passports	
Visas	
Health and travel insurance policies*	
Photocopies of important documents*	

* Leave originals with your family.

Special airline meals

If you have specific dietary needs, you can request special meals on airline flights. Some of the special meals include a fruit plate or kosher vegetarian (Moslem), vegetarian (Hindu), diabetic (low sugar). Ask your travel agent to arrange any special meals that you might need.

Traveler's health history

When you travel internationally, you should carry a list of the following information:

- Your current medications, including trade name, generic name, and dosage. (Also: current prescriptions)
- Any medical conditions, especially for long flights where illness could occur and there might be no doctor on the flight. Medical conditions might include hypertension, diabetes, or heart problems.
- Your known drug allergies.
- Name and telephone number of your regular physician.
- Name and telephone number of a relative or friend in the United States to assist in the event you become ill while traveling.

Traveler's medical kit

A medical kit may be critical for travelers who have health problems. You might want to consult with your doctor to determine the need for specific medication. Your kit might include:

- Prescription drugs such as antidiarrhea medications, motion sickness drugs, sleeping pills, or melatonin to combat jet lag.
- Nonprescription drugs, such as aspirin, antihistamine/decongestant (cold remedy), Pepto-Bismol or Tums for an upset stomach, and Dramamine or ginger for motion sickness.

En route to your destination

When people come to the United States from another country, it usually means flying. If you come from an Asian country, the flight may take fifteen to twenty hours depending on the number of stopovers and your final destination. In my case, coming from the Philippines to Washington, DC, took eighteen hours of flight time, not counting the hours waiting for connecting flights. As a transient, you customarily stay at the airport until you are ready to board your next flight. It is tiring to wait, but the good thing is it gives you the opportunity to stretch, get something decent to eat, visit the stores, and walk around.

Once you reach your destination, if friends or relatives are there to meet you, you do not have to worry about taking public transportation (subway, train, taxi, or bus). Arriving for the first time in the United States may make you nervous, especially if you have to take public transportation and cannot speak English. One thing you can do is to check with Traveler's Aid to ask if they can write in English where you are going. If the person at the desk does not understand your language, it will be a tough situation. You can try and see if other people at the airport can help you in your own language. Most Americans do not speak other languages; though if they do, Spanish is the most common second language.

It is easier if you are going to a hotel, because all you need is the name and address of the hotel for a taxi driver to take you there. If you are taking a bus, navigation is an entirely different problem, so it would be helpful to get bus schedules or maps in advance.

Another common option is to ask a bilingual flight attendant all your questions before you land. If the flight attendant cannot answer your questions, he or she can often give you further instructions on what to do and where to go when you arrive at the airport.

Traveler's Aid

Traveler's Aid runs information counters at major airports and assists stranded and otherwise troubled travelers. You might want to visit the Traveler's Aid desk or station if you have questions, no matter how simple they might seem. They might still direct you to talk to other people, but at least you do not have to roam around and lose time in the process, especially if you have only a short time before you board your next flight.

On one of my trips from Washington, DC to San Francisco, several years ago, my daughter and I were sitting at the airport waiting for our flight. The plane we were supposed to take was many hours late because of mechanical problems, and another plane was not available.

An Asian man who spoke no English kept following us around. When we got up to look for a place to eat, he, too, got up and closely followed us. Every time we moved to another seat, he rose up also, followed us, and took a seat near us.

We felt sorry for him, but having him follow us around wherever we went became annoying after a while. What was interesting was that he stayed close to us as if we could help him. Perhaps, since we looked Asian, as he did, he felt assured that he was in good company.

When the airline personnel finally announced that our plane was arriving, the man approached me, took out a translation book and a piece of paper from his bag and wrote in English, "Help call relative." Remembering my own earlier telephone experience, I dialed the number he gave me and asked the operator to call collect, but unfortunately no one answered the phone. In my last attempt to help him, I took him to a Traveler's Aid station.

You can always find good Samaritans around who are willing to help people in need, but on many occasions, it is difficult for a traveler who cannot speak English. That is why it is important to have all the information you need before you leave your home country. This information is essential in case you are stuck in an airport and need to call the person who is supposed to meet you to say that you will be coming in on another flight. Always be prepared for contingencies.

Making the most of your layovers

When you come from as far as Asia or Africa, you may have several layovers while waiting for your connecting flights. Having these stops gives you more of a chance to stretch or walk around; airports offer many services, especially the bigger airports. Some of the offerings could be health clubs where you can have massages, facilities such as hair salons, postal offices, hot showers, shoeshine stands, duty-free stores, and Internet terminals.

Getting Through Immigration and Customs

When you leave your home country to emigrate to the United States, you must know what immigration and customs officials expect from you at your port of entry. You might find it overwhelming if it is your first trip abroad. You may also be nervous once the process starts—from finding yourself in long lines waiting your turn to be interrogated by an immigration officer, to having to open your suitcase(s) for customs inspection. Don't accept or carry packages from anyone unless you open them and examine the contents. Often, customs inspectors scrutinize the contents of suitcases and open sealed packages for examination. You will be asked before you board the plane if you are carrying anything you didn't pack yourself or that anyone unknown to you gave you to carry. If you answer yes, the security people will open your luggage to search for bombs.

Immigration inspection

On entering the United States, you proceed to the immigration section where your documents are processed for entry. This is when you provide your passport. After processing, you are given an I-94 card. It will be stamped with the dates showing your authorized stay. Each time you exit and reenter the United States, you receive another I-94 card with a new period of authorized stay.

If you are an immigrant, you may have certain restrictions dictated by the terms of your residency permit. If you are a non-immigrant (tourist, student, contract laborer), you must pass through a more thorough inspection to ensure that you are entering the country legally. An immigration officer will ask to see your passport in order to check your identity and stamp the I-94 card (which accompanies your passport) with the date and location of your entry or reentry (if you had previously visited the United States).

Although answering questions may be tedious, especially if you arrive in the early hours of the morning feeling jet-lagged, you must make every effort to respond politely and accurately to the questions. It is against the law to make a false statement to an immigration officer, and it is likely to delay your processing if an immigration officer becomes suspicious.

Based on my observations from having entered and left America many times, tourists seem to be scrutinized more than the immigrants. Having passed through the immigration line once as a tourist, I remember the questions that were typically asked by immigration officers:

- What is your purpose in coming here?
- How long do you plan to stay?
- What city or state are you going to reside in?
- Who are you visiting?
- Do you have any relatives or friends living in America? (If you say yes, you are asked further: Who they are and where they are located.)
- How much money do you have with you?

Of course, not everyone is asked these detailed questions. The questions depend on the credibility of the documents immigrants carry with them. Questions to non-immigrants—students, contract laborers, those with work permits, and those with business visas—are less complicated because these people come with clear, firm purposes—to study, to work as contract laborers or domestic help, or to start a business.

Customs inspection

After you clear immigration, you will proceed to customs. The U.S. Customs Service has the dual responsibility of keeping prohibited items out of the United States and ensuring that all duties and taxes are paid on imported items. The U.S. Department of Agriculture restricts the type and amount of plant and animal products you can bring into the country, and all such products are subject to inspection. The purpose for interviews and inspections is to prevent the spread of animal- and plant-borne diseases, but they also are used to prevent trafficking in endangered or threatened species. Customs inspectors also want to prevent smuggling of illegal drugs.

When your plane is close to arriving in the United States, flight attendants will distribute customs declaration forms to be completed by all passengers. If you are traveling as a family, whoever is the head of the family fills it out. The questions you have to answer include the number of people in your party (if you are traveling as a family), the items you are bringing, and their value. Completing the form is the first step in the customs process. As you go through customs, an inspector interviews you, takes your written declaration form, and determines whether further inspection of your bags is necessary.

Most inspections are simple and usually involve a customs inspector opening only one or two bags for inspection. More complicated inspections can include a detailed search of everything you are carrying and wearing. The final step in the inspection process is paying any duties, taxes, or fines that you may owe.

There are separate lines at customs inspection: those who have things to declare and those who have nothing to declare. This separation has become convenient for travelers who have only a suitcase or two and nothing to declare, so they can move through quickly. They need only present the customs inspection form they completed while on the plane.

After the customs officer checks and signs your customs declaration form and gives you the nod, you can proceed to the baggage area to pick up your suitcases.

You have very few rights during a customs inspection. If you are delayed by the customs inspection and miss your connecting flights, you have no recourse against the U.S. government. On the other hand, if you explain your predicament to the airline it is likely they will allow you to take a later flight without any penalty.

Getting Around in the United States

Once you reach your destination, you have to know how to find your way around. If you do not have friends or relatives to show you around, renting a car is an option. But if you cannot speak English, driving will be doubly difficult. Even if you speak some English, you may not know how to read a map accurately. Some immigrants may ask a friend or relative in America to send them maps to study in advance, but this is rarely done. They would rather rely on friends or relatives to guide them. If you are renting a car, do not hesitate to stop and try to get directions, even if you think your English is not good.

Depending on which country you come from, driving habits may be different. People in the United States drive on the right-hand side of the road, the opposite side from England, Hong Kong, Ireland, Japan, New Zealand, the Bahamas, and most Caribbean Islands. U.S. highways have dividing lines that cars must stay within, unlike in some countries where you have no lines and few rules. Ignorance of the law will not prevent you from receiving a ticket.

Another thing to remember is that littering is against the law and may result in a large fine.

Feeling at home in America

New arrivals like to feel at home when they first come to America. In my case, the very first place I visited was Chinatown in New York City. I remember roaming the streets of Chinatown in the snow on my first day after I got off the plane. What I distinctly recall is that everyone wore familiar clothes, spoke the various Chinese dialects, and ate Chinese food. If you are among others that share your heritage, you will feel safer and more at ease.

The Chinatowns in America offer living testimony that there are places immigrants could call "home away from home." There are also "Little Italys," which huddle close to the water in Boston, New York, New Haven, Philadelphia, and Baltimore. I visited Little Italy in New York several years ago. As I walked from restaurant to restaurant, I sensed the close-knit, friendly Italian groups. The food was superb and the ambiance warm and comfortable.

Other than Chinatowns and Little Italys, there are also collections of ethnic and folk arts that are the best reflection of an area's diverse culture. For instance, paintings by Cuban and other Hispanic artists hang in the Florida Museum of Hispanic and Latin American art in Miami's Buena Vista neighborhood. Cubans are known for their wood carvings and embroidered shirts called "guyaberas." Handmade boats and sails are a Caribbean specialty, while the people of Florida's Greek community are known for making seafaring gear.

A number of "Korea towns" are also growing rapidly, especially along the East Coast. You can find Korean grocery stores and restaurants in most major cities. Times are changing fast. You are now able to buy familiar spices that you used to order from your home country because they were not available in America.

Currency exchanges

Typically, you will want to ensure that a certain amount of your travel money is exchanged to U.S. dollars while you are still in your home country. You can exchange your money through banks, government change offices, or currency exchange stations located at airports. Before you leave the airport be sure to exchange enough currency to last for a few days. Most American banks are not set up for fast currency exchanges, and some may take several days to complete any type of currency exchange.

Most American and foreign banks will exchange local currencies to U.S. dollars, but in some countries there are limits of $500 to $1,000 per traveler. Because of these limits, people sometimes resort to the black market where they can easily exchange greater amounts of money in their local currencies to U.S. dollars without problems, especially if they are tourists. You should exchange most of your currency once you arrive in the United States because the rate of exchange is usually better here than in your country of origin.

Another option is to open a savings account in U.S. dollars in your home country, as more and more foreign nationals are doing. By this means, a member of your family back home can deposit money to your account while you are in the United States. The easy way to deposit and withdraw money is to have a joint account with a family member.

Tipping

Tipping is practiced in most countries. The only difference is how much and at what rate. What percentage do you tip waiters in restaurants, baggage handlers, valet parking attendants, and taxi drivers—just to name a few of the service-related jobs.

In a restaurant, the amount of the tip should relate to the quality of service and the cost of the food served. You should not be forced to give the standard tip if you are not satisfied with the service and food. Some restaurants automatically add a tip for large groups. Even so, if the service is bad, you should ask the manager to deduct the tip from the bill. Tipping should be determined by the customer. But some waiters bothered by bad tips like the idea of automatically adding the tip to a customer's bill.

Table 10 lists recommended tipping amounts for America.[15]

Table 10 - Tipping Standards in America

Service	Standard tip
HOTELS	
Desk clerk	None unless special service is given during long stay; then, $5
Concierge	Between $5 to $10 average. More for special services or favors
Room service waiter	15 percent of bill
Bell hop	$5 - $10 for bringing your luggage to your room
RESTAURANTS	
Coffee shop and counter services wait staff	Between 8 percent to 10 percent of the bill
Full service restaurants	15 percent of the bill before sales tax
Fine restaurants where the staff is large and shares the tips	Between 15 percent and 20 percent
Upscale restaurants in metropolitan areas	20 percent is typical
Bartender	10 to 15 percent of bar bill
Coat check attendant	$1 - $2 for each coat
Rest room attendant (if any)	50 cents - $1.00
Valet or car park attendant	$1 (more if the car is an expensive model)
AIRPORTS	
Car-rental shuttle driver who helps with your suitcase	$1 to $2
Taxi driver	15 percent of fare—no less than 25 cents
Limousine driver	20 percent of bill
Skycap (Baggage handler at airports)	$1 or more per suitcase
TRAINS	
Dining car waiter	15 percent of bill
Stewards/car waiter	15 percent of bar bill
Redcap (service available at major stations to carry your luggage to the train)	Service is usually provided free, but most passengers tip a redcap $1 a bag

Sources: Web sites *www.tipping.org* and *www.channel2000.com.*

11. Housing Options

When immigrants arrive in America, renting an apartment, a condominium, or a house is often their first consideration. Many stay with friends or relatives for a short time until they find an appropriate place they can call home. Buying is a decision usually put off for the future.

Most choose to rent first because they do not know whether the location they first settle in is where they want to live permanently. In most cases, the first place immigrants settle in is a stepping stone until they have gained enough job experience, saved enough money, and can look for better opportunities elsewhere.

Deciding Where to Live

Deciding where to live takes serious consideration. You should look at your situation first and see who will be affected by your decision, especially if you have a family. Climate is only one factor. Other considerations include the opportunity to find better-paying jobs in your areas of expertise, good public or private schools for your children, and close proximity to friends and relatives from whom you may feel comfortable getting support in your first few years in America.

Most of the people who talked to me prefer to live in an area of the United States that has a climate similar to where they come from. Their choices of where to live also depended on other factors such as job opportunities and close proximity to family or friends who are already in America. Many preferred larger cities, such as Boston, Chicago, New York, or San Francisco, where they know they can get better-paying jobs.

City or suburbs

Once you have selected a city or state, another consideration is whether to live in the city or the outlying suburban areas. If you lived in a city in your home country, you may also be more comfortable living in a city when in America, especially if you do not own a car. But you may decide to live in the suburbs if you have young children and do not need access to buses and other forms of public transportation.

If you want privacy and security for your family, you might prefer to find an apartment or a house in the countryside or suburban areas. One thing you might do is check with the Housing and Urban Development (HUD) counseling center closest to you to get information about average selling prices and rental payments in different parts of the country. There are HUD offices around the country, and they are a good source of information about the local housing market.

You also should think about work-related considerations. How much time would it take you or your spouse to commute to and from work? Ideally, your commute should take, at most, less than an hour, especially if you have "latchkey" children—those who come home to an empty house after school.

If you have children

Sooner or later, all kids need to learn some independence but it is not surprising that many parents look for help in deciding whether and when their children can be safe when no adults are around. A good practice is to have a "what-if" drill with your kids, with a contingency plan for each situation.

For example, what if: They come home to find the front door already open? They lose their key? The smoke alarm goes off? There is a power failure? Someone knocks on the door asking to use the phone? Someone calls and wants to know if mom or dad is home?

In addition to having contingency plans for each situation, you should set up rules that kids can understand and agree to in advance. Some of these rules could be that they have to do their homework once they get home, which household appliances they can use, and guidelines for using the phone, computer, or TV, or even going to a friend's house after they finish their homework.

If you are not comfortable leaving your children alone to fend for themselves for a few hours while you are still at work, you may want to take advantage of after-school programs. Such programs allow your children to do homework while waiting to be picked up. If you have parents living with you, arrange for them to watch your children a few hours each day.

Many states have laws against leaving young children unattended. You should check with your local authorities if you are unsure of the laws in your area.

Renting

Most immigrants rent for several years before they can afford to buy a house. Many rent apartments because they are usually more affordable than houses. If you have a big family, you might have no choice but to rent a house. Renting gives you the advantage of paying a lower monthly payment and saving the extra money for a down payment on a house.

Dave Lang still rents an apartment even though he has lived in America for ten years. He picked an apartment in Arlington, Virginia, because of proximity to his friends and convenience to many places, such as grocery and video stores. Dave does not plan to buy a house within the next five years because he and his wife are thinking about moving back to Vietnam, or possibly living in both countries, spending six months there, six months in America.

When Lina was single, she rented an apartment close to work. That allowed her more time to sleep late since her place was only a few blocks from the office. She tended to walk to and from work and to go home for lunch, which helped her save a lot of money on food and transportation. The close distance offered another advantage for her because she was able to be more flexible in her working hours. She could work long hours without worrying about bus schedules. Since Lina lived close to restaurants, clubs, and theaters, her weekdays were always full. The only drawback was that her rent was more expensive in the city than it would have been in the suburbs. What she could afford to pay was only enough for an efficiency or a one-bedroom apartment.

The advantages of renting instead of buying are:

- Renting requires less advance planning compared to purchasing.

- You are not responsible for the costs of routine repairs and maintenance.
- You can easily move out when your lease expires.

Buying

Buying a house is a personal, individual decision that depends on many factors, but primarily on the availability of money. Can you afford to buy a house at this time? Do you have enough money for a down payment? Closing costs? Other incidentals? Buying a house is a serious investment.

But once you are ready to buy a house, it is progress for you, as well as for most Americans. Buying a house is something to be proud of. You own it. It's yours. And you are more inspired to decorate it and buy nice things for your own place.

Lina Shoobridge bought a house in 1985 with her first husband and again in 1996 with her second husband. When she bought a house the first time, it was for investment purposes, although the marriage ended too soon for anyone to make money from the investment. After her first marriage ended (while Lina and her husband were living in London), Lina came to America for a visit. She reapplied at the World Bank and the International Monetary Fund (IMF), took the necessary exams, and went back to England to wait for job openings. Six months later, she was offered a job at the IMF. After a few months, her boyfriend from England decided to join her in America to get married. Lina and her second husband bought a house primarily for the sake of their children, giving them room to play and a backyard. Privacy and the enjoyment of having a backyard with a garden are good for the family.

Housing, whether to buy or to rent, is a decision usually taken seriously by everyone, especially by immigrants. However, buying a home should not be decided based only on economics. You should also take into consideration social and emotional factors, such as your:

- Desire for privacy.
- Feeling proud to finally own a property.

- Willingness to commute if you cannot afford to buy a house convenient to everything.
- Ability to take care of minor or major repairs on the house, which are realities you face as a homeowner.

Other than your monthly mortgage, you should also put money away for contingencies, which could include unavoidable and unplanned repairs, such as plumbing problems or an appliance breaking down.

When shopping for a house, consider the location. Following are several techniques you might want to consider:

- Decide on the neighborhood you might want to live in by visiting areas you prefer and talking to residents about their experiences living in the area. Ideally, your best resource may be a real estate agent who can concentrate on your needs.
- Get an idea of prices of houses in the neighborhood through your real estate agent, who can easily obtain this information. Or, you can check newspaper advertisements or real estate guides for prices of houses.
- Whether the house you are thinking of buying is in the city or in the suburbs, check out the schools, real estate taxes, houses of worship, shopping facilities, public transportation, and other amenities.

Advantages of home ownership

Think about the following advantages of owning a house. You should buy a house because of its rewards and because it is important to you.

A sound investment. When you carefully choose a house you can afford, the payoff is great. Each time you make a mortgage payment, you are building equity in your house. It is a nest egg. Equity is the portion of the resale proceeds that you get to keep after the mortgage balance is deducted. The longer you live in your house, the greater your equity. Unlike most of the material things you buy, a house can actually increase in value as time passes. In inflationary times, especially, the dollar value of your house usually increases.

Satisfaction and security. Owning your own home brings a happy feeling. As a homeowner, you can decorate and improve the house any way you like. It can also give you a new sense of pride in your surroundings. You and your family will become a part of a new community.

Disadvantages of home ownership

It is easy to get caught up in your emotions and the excitement of buying a house and forget that you may have problems too. Following are a few disadvantages.

High costs. Other than making the mortgage payments, costs will most likely be higher than rent; and you will have additional costs for repairs and maintenance of the house.

Ties up cash. Your house might increase in value as time passes, but you should not count on getting a big return on your investment right away. If you should sell your house during the first few years of owning it, you are likely to lose money because the value of your house may not appreciate enough to cover the closing costs, moving expenses, and the five to seven percent commission that goes to the real estate agent.

Tougher moves. After you buy your house, you may not have as much flexibility to choose a new location or job. This drawback may be more difficult for immigrants.

No guarantees. Again, there is no guarantee that the house you own will appreciate in value, particularly during the first few years and even if you own it for years. In the first few years, you are mostly paying the interest on the mortgage loan; very little of your monthly payments go toward the principal, yet repaying the principal is how you build your equity. However, equity also increases when the value of your house increases.

Shopping for a house

If you decide you want to buy a house, check out the steps you need to take. There is no right way to buy a house. The exact steps vary depending on the kind of house you plan to buy, where you want to buy, and how much money you can afford to spend. When the decision is a "go," the next steps are to find a real estate agent; prequalify for a loan; begin house hunting; find a real estate attorney (if needed); inspect the house, grounds and neighborhood; make an offer and sign a purchase contract; get professional inspections; apply for a mortgage; do a final walk-through; and then close the sale. By this time, you are set and ready to move in.

Epilogue

In his book, *Migrations and Cultures,* Thomas Sowell writes, "In a world of 100 million immigrants—19 million of them refugees—migration is a major social phenomenon, as it has been for thousands of years." Sowell adds, "Differences among peoples and among places lie at the heart of migrations. Moving has many and often heavy costs, including not simply the financial cost of transportation itself or even the additional expenses that go with searching for new work and new homes." [16]

Today, thousands of people continue to emigrate to the United States from all over the world. Most emigrate primarily for economic and social reasons: to explore or visit, study, work, start a business, or get married. Many come because they can. New immigration laws have helped those who are eligible to get visas through sponsorship by their families.

The United States today is more integrated than ever. Increasingly we are sharing neighborhoods, school, work, social activities, religious life, and even love and marriage across racial lines. More than ever, we are enjoying each other's company and distinctive cultures. Global society, where there are networks of business and communications, draws us closer and brings valuable rewards to an enriching diversity. Diverse backgrounds and talents are helping America be what it is today. This increasing diversity makes living in America more exciting, more enjoyable, and more meaningful.

The experiences of the people interviewed for this book have been a mix of good fortune and many obstacles, which, through hard work, they have overcome. If they were to turn back their clocks and start over, would they have done things differently? In many ways, yes. There were a number of things they were not prepared for and learned about only when they set foot in America. But those were lessons learned that will forever stay in their minds and hearts. They had no regrets or resentment, despite the often painful transition. They were happy for the opportunity to make a new life for themselves and their families, which could not have happened had they stayed in their home countries.

It is interesting that the people interviewed for this book remembered and so willingly talked about their embarrassing experiences during their early years in America. They seemed to enjoy talking and laughing about their own naïveté, as if these experiences had happened only yesterday instead of years ago. If they had learned more about America's history, culture, and lifestyle before coming here they would not have fumbled the way they did. But they realize now that those fumbles were just learning experiences and part of their road to success.

Appendix A. Support Groups and Multicultural Resources

Support Groups

Center for Education, Employment and Community (CEEC)
55 Chapel Street
Newton, MA 02158-1060
(617) 969-7100; (617) 332-4318 (fax)
E-mail: *VivianG@edc.org*

Center for Education, Employment and Community works for the economic and social well-being of all. CEEC brings together people of diverse talents and backgrounds to create systems that help students achieve high standards, workers advance in their careers, and citizens improve their communities. CEEC is part of the Education Development Center, Inc. (EDC). EDC is committed to education that builds knowledge and skills, makes possible a deeper understanding of the world, and engages learners as active, problem-solving participants.

The American Immigration Network (AIN)
Web site: *www.usavisanow.com*

The American Immigration Network provides U.S. immigration assistance, for both individuals and businesses, by a team of experienced, licensed immigration attorneys. They also offer the "Do It Yourself U.S. Immigration Kit," an inexpensive ($49.95) alternative to retaining an attorney. Each kit contains all of the necessary forms, sample forms, sample letters, easy-to-understand instructions, government agency addresses and phone numbers, and much more.

National Neighborhood Coalition (NNC)
Web site: *www.neighborhoodcoalition.org*

National Neighborhood Coalition serves as the national voice for neighborhoods by providing a crucial link to Washington for neighborhood and community-based organizations. NNC fosters communication and collaboration among local, regional, and national organizations working to build healthy and sustainable communities.

NNC also promotes public policies that strengthen the role of community and neighborhood-based nonprofits as problem solvers and community builders.

Multicultural Organizations

Following are some organizations to contact over issues with discrimination and racism. Be aware that many organizations take several weeks or longer to respond to inquiries, so allow as much time as possible.

Intercultural Mutual Assistance Association (IMAA)
"Building Bridges Between Cultures"
16 Seventh Avenue, SW
Rochester, MN 55902
(507) 289-5960; (507) 289-6199 (fax)
E-mail: *imaa@sparc.isl.net*
Web site: *www.vietline.com/imaa*

The Intercultural Mutual Assistance Association provides services in twelve languages and provides support in self-sufficiency employment, youth and family crime prevention, social adjustment, community development information and referral, volunteer services, and immigration assistance.

African Americans for Humanism (AAH)
Box 664
Buffalo, NY 14226
(716) 636-7571

African Americans for Humanism is dedicated to developing humanism in the African-American community through outreach to those who are unchurched. This group is especially concerned with fighting racism through humanistic education. It publishes the quarterly newsletter *AAH Examiner*.

American-Arab Anti-Discrimination Committee
4201 Connecticut Avenue, NW, Suite 500
Washington, DC 20008
(202) 244-2990

American-Arab Anti-Discrimination Committee fights anti-Arab stereotyping in the media and discrimination and hate crimes against Arab-Americans. It publishes a series of issue papers and a number of books.

Hispanic Policy Development Project (HPDP)
1001 Connecticut Avenue, NW
Washington, DC 20036
(202) 822-8414

Hispanic Policy Development Project is a nonprofit organization that encourages analysis of public policies affecting Hispanic youth in the United States, especially in education, employment, and family issues. It publishes a number of books and pamphlets, including *Together Is Better: Building Strong Partnerships Between Schools and Hispanic Parents.*

National MultiCultural Institute (NMCI)
3000 Connecticut Avenue, NW, Suite 438
Washington, DC 20008-2556
Web site: *www.nmci.org*
(202) 483-0700; (202) 483-5233 (fax)

National MultiCultural Institute is a private, nonprofit organization funded through fees for service, contracts, foundation grants, and corporate and individual contributions. Its mission is to increase communication, understand and respect people from different racial, ethnic, and cultural backgrounds, and provide a forum for discussion of the critical issues of multiculturalism facing American society.

Books on Multiculturalism

Multicultural Citizenship: A Liberal Theory of Minority Rights
Will Kymlicka, Oxford University Press, 1996
Price: $19.95. ISBN: 0198290918.

Multicultural Citizenship: A Liberal Theory of Minority Rights aims to resolve the tension between liberalism and group rights by contending that individuals must exist within a 'societal culture' in order to express their political and cultural identity. Chapters that may be of interest are: Chapter 6, *Justice and Minority Rights*, Chapter 7, *Ensuring a Voice for Minorities*, and Chapter 8, *Toleration and Its Limits.*

Survival Kit for Multicultural Living
Ellen Summerfield, Intercultural Press, 1997
Price: $16.96, ISBN: 1877864498.

Survival Kit for Multicultural Living features children from all over the world. They look, speak, and do things differently but inside they are just like any other children.

We Are All Multiculturalists Now
Nathan Glazer, Harvard University Press, 1998
Price: $12.95, ISBN: 067494836X.

We Are All Multiculturalists Now concludes that it seems we must pass through a period in which we recognize differences, we celebrate differences, we turn the spotlight on the inadequacies in the integration of our minorities in our past and present, and we raise up for special consideration the achievements of our minorities.

Whoever You Are
Mem Fox and Leslie Staub, Harcourt Brace, 1997
Price: $16.00, ISBN: 0152007873.

Whoever You Are explains that despite the differences between people around the world, there are similarities that join us together, which include common experiences such as pain, joy, and love.

Ethnic Associations

Ethnic Cultural Preservation Council (ECPC)
6500 S. Pulaski Road
Chicago, Illinois 60629
(312) 582-5143

Ethnic Cultural Preservation Council is a coalition of ethnic and other kinds of museums, historical societies, libraries, archives, and cultural centers. The council's purpose is to facilitate development of arts and humanities programs and to sponsor seminars, exhibits, and the dissemination of information on ethnic activities.

National Center for Urban Ethnic Affairs
P.O. Box 20
Washington, DC 20064
(202) 232-3600

National Center for Urban Ethnic Affairs, affiliated with the United States Catholic Conference, develops neighborhood programs and policies that promote appreciation of ethnic cultural diversity nationwide.

Diversity Programs

One America
Web site: *www.whitehouse.gov/Initiatives*

One America is one of many programs working to encourage participation of people from various racial backgrounds and to ensure opportunities for all Americans. Promising Practices highlights efforts designed to improve race relations to build One America.

A WORLD OF DIFFERENCE Institute
Contact your ADL Regional Office, ADL National Headquarters
(212) 885-7700
Web site: *www.adl.org*

A World of Difference Institute is for people who share a community—be it a school, workplace, neighborhood, or campus. The program started in Boston in 1985 when the Anti-Defamation League (ADL) and WCVB-TV joined together to fight prejudice. From the start, they embraced this remarkably effective way to promote and appreciate diversity. It changed hearts and minds, and it quickly spread across the nation—and beyond.

All One Heart
Promoting Diversity Tolerance Through Education
12190 Perris Blvd., Suite F-141
Moreno Valley, CA 92557
Web site: *www.alloneheart.com*

All One Heart is an online forum where visitors are automatically respected and loved, without negative judgments being made about anyone based upon physical attributes or appearance. The focus is on similarities and on educating and celebrating each other's diversity.

American Institute for Managing Diversity, Inc.
50 Hurt Plaza, Suite 1150
Atlanta, GA 30303
(404) 302-9226
Web site: *www.aimd.org*

American Institute for Managing Diversity, Inc., offers profiles in diversity, research studies on diversity, educational services, Internet resources, and other programs.

Bridge Builders®
P.O. Box 240487
Memphis, TN 38124
(901) 452-5600
Web site: *www.bridgesinc.org*

If you come to the United States with children who are entering high school, there is a landmark program that will be beneficial to them. In this program, Bridge Builders®, students are being prepared for future responsibilities in a multicultural world. As its charter, Bridge Builders® brings together high school students of diverse backgrounds and gives them training in leadership, human relations, and civic responsibility. Through this training, students are able to move beyond the traditional barriers of race, religion, culture, or class and see themselves as a community.

Bridging the Gap Project, Inc.
1717 S. Chestnut
Fresno, CA 93702
(559) 453-2245
Web site: *www.fresno.edu*

Bridging the Gap Project, Inc., is a project at Clarkston High School in Clarkston, Michigan, that looks at conflict among high school students, and between high school students and their refugee parents. Such conflict affects everyone working with these refugees, and includes a substantial amount of hate crime from unknown persons. The refugee groups affected are Iraqi, Somali, Bosnian, and Vietnamese. The local community is largely Euro-American and African-American.

National Association of Gender Diversity Training
(480) 473-0426; (480) 473-0427 (fax)
E-mail: *info@gendertraining.com*
Web site: *www.gendertraining.com*

National Association of Gender Diversity Training assists individuals and businesses in creating a workplace culture of understanding, respect, and harmony between men and women. It also provides services that promote continued improvement and excellence in gender communication and equity for all people.

National Coalition Building Institute (NCBI)
1120 Connecticut Avenue, NW, Suite 450
Washington, DC 20036
(202) 785-9400; (202) 785-3385 (fax)
Web site: *www.ncbi.org*

National Coalition Building Institute is a nonprofit organization offering programs to reduce prejudice and build team environments in the workplace.

Rainbow Child International
Box 1180
Bryn Mawr, PA 19010
(610) 520-9937
Web site: *www.rainbowchild.com*

Rainbow Child International is a nonprofit organization building global and environmental awareness and respect for cultural diversity. It offers the World Wisdom Multicultural Arts Programs, which are designed to defuse barriers, misunderstanding and fear between people of different cultural backgrounds. It also offers The World Wisdom Cultural Arts Programs and Materials, which are tailored for preschool to adult audiences. The fun activities include international dance, storytelling, music, ecology, performance, and workshops.

Books on Diversity

No Mountain High Enough: Secrets of Successful African American Women
Dorothy Ehrhart-Morrison, Conari Press, 1997
Price: $11.96. ISBN: 0943233984.

No Mountain High Enough profiles thirty-two successful black women, from judges to rocket scientists to corporate executive officers, revealing the combination of hard work, determination, and the support of family that drove them forward against the odds.

Working Together: Producing Synergy by Honoring Diversity
Angeles Cerrien, et al., New Leaders Press, 1998
Price: $28.00, ISBN: 188670023.

Working Together looks at diversity as an advantage to be used, not a problem to be solved. Key topics include building the foundation for a partnership, getting to know you, bridging the gap, and living and loving in a diverse world.

Community Relations Organizations

Community Relations Service (CRS)
U.S. Department of Justice
Second and Chestnut Street, #208
Philadelphia, PA 19106
(215) 597-2344

Community Relations Services, created by the Civil Rights Act of 1965, helps prevent and resolve community-wide conflict based on race, color, and national origin. Its staff provides mediation and conciliation, technical assistance, training for law enforcement personnel, public education and awareness, and contingency planning for potentially provocative events.

Office for Victims of Crime
U.S. Department of Justice
810 Seventh St., NW
Washington, DC 20531
(202) 307-5983

Office for Victims of Crime, Department of Justice, gives grants to states to provide victim assistance and victim compensation in the event of a hate crime. Upon the request of a state, the office sends out a response from one of its eight regional offices.

The Peace Center
Education in Conflict Resolution and Violence Prevention
102 West Maple Avenue
Langhorne, PA 19047-2820
(215) 750-7220; (215) 750-9237 (fax)
E-mail: *peace@comcat.com*

The Peace Center has worked for community peace and social justice since 1982. Its programs are designed to help reduce violence and conflict in schools, homes, and communities through a multicultural, community-based approach.

Victims Information Line
(800) 563-0808

Victims Information Line is a hotline number you can call to report a hate crime incident. Whether you are the victim of or a witness to a hate crime, information about you is kept confidential.

Appendix B. Government and Educational Resources

Government Agencies

Department of Commerce (DOC)
14th Street between Constitution Avenue and E Street, NW
Washington, DC 20230
(202) 377-2000

Department of Commerce promotes international trade, economic growth, and the technological advancement of American business. DOC collects information on economic statistics, grants, and patents, registers trademarks, and assists in the growth of minority businesses.

Department of Education
Web site: *http://ed.gov*

U.S. Department of Education links to the best starting points on a variety of educational topics, such as after-school programs, bilingual education, community learning centers, and many more.

Department of Justice, Community Relations Service
5550 Friendship Blvd.
Chevy Chase, MD 20815
(301) 492-5929

Department of Justice, Community Relations Service Division, provides on-site resolution by conciliation specialists of any dispute relating to discrimination on the basis of race, color, or national origin.

Department of Justice, Civil Rights Division
10th Street and Pennsylvania Avenue, NW
Washington, DC 20530
(202) 514-4224

Department of Justice, Civil Rights Division is responsible for enforcing federal civil rights laws that prohibit discrimination. The Civil Rights Division coordinates the efforts of federal executive agencies and departments to eliminate discrimination in programs conducted by the federal government or that receive federal assistance.

Equal Employment Opportunity Commission (EEOC)
1801 L Street, NW
Washington, DC 20507
(800) USA-EEOC or (202) 663-4900

Equal Employment Opportunity Commission eliminates discrimination in employment. You can obtain a copy of the National Enforcement Plan by accessing the Web site above. To be automatically connected with the nearest EEOC field office, call (800) 669-4000 or visit the Web site: *www.eeoc.gov*.

Immigration and Naturalization Service (INS)
Department of Justice
425 I Street, NW
Washington, DC 20536
(205) 514-4316

Immigration and Naturalization Services administers and enforces immigration laws. It also operates four regional and thirty-three district offices in the United States, and three abroad.

Legal Services Corporation (LSC)
400 Virginia Avenue, SW
Washington, DC 20024
(202) 863-1820

Legal Services Corporation is a quasi-governmental agency that makes quality legal assistance available for noncriminal proceedings to those who would otherwise be unable to afford counsel.

Library of Congress
Web site: *www.loc.gov*

The Library of Congress has the most extensive collection of books. You can read about American history, the workings of the American government, civil rights, local and federal government at the macro level, and find out how to integrate into society.

Note: You can visit and use the resources but you cannot actually borrow books from the Library of Congress.

Small Business Administration (SBA)
409 Third Street, NW
Washington, DC 20476
(202) 205-6600 or (800) U-ASK-SBA
Web site: *www.sbaonline.sba.gov*

The Small Business Administration represents small business interests in Congress; provides information, referral, and educational services directly to small businesses; facilitates the processing of grants and loans to small businesses; helps small businesses obtain government contracts to provide goods and services; and assists in the development of small businesses owned by women and minorities.

U.S. Small Business Administration
Office of Women's Business Ownership
409 Third Street, SW
Sixth Floor
Washington, DC 20416
(202) 205-6673; (202) 205-7230 (fax)

The U.S. Small Business Administration Office of Women's Business Ownership is an umbrella group under the Small Business Administration that establishes long-term training and counseling centers. They provide technical and financial assistance to assist small businesses owned by women in their start-up and expansion.

Academic Associations

American Association of University Professors
Web site: *www.aaup.org*

American Association of University Professors defends academic freedom and tenure, advocates collegial governance, and develops policies ensuring due process.

The Association of Academic Health Centers (AHC)
Web site: *www.ahcnet.org*

The Center of Academic Health Centers is a national, nonprofit organization that consists of over 100 institutional members throughout the United States that are the health complexes of the major universities. AHC consists of an allopathic or osteopathic school of medicine, at least one other health professions school, and one or more teaching hospitals.

The Center for Development and Learning (CDL)
Web site: *www.cdl.org*

The Center for Development and Learning is a nonprofit organization whose purpose is to help all children break the cycle of failure to achieve school and lifetime success. CDL is founded on the premise that although all children learn differently, every child wants to learn, every child can learn, and every child deserves to learn in ways that improve their chances for success. CDL's goal is to activate and achieve sweeping change in the way all children are taught.

Directories of Colleges and Universities

American Association of Community Colleges (AACC)
One Dupont Circle, NW, Suite 410
Washington, DC 20035
Web site: *www.aacc.nche.edu*

American Association of Community Colleges provides extensive information on community colleges nationwide. Other information is provided on Educational Services, Grant Information, and Additional Resources such as Higher Education Cooperative Purchase Consortium and the ERIC Clearinghouse for Community Colleges.

American Universities
Web site: *www.globalcomputing.com*

American Universities is a site that provides school listings throughout the United States for all 50 states.

Scholarships and Financial Aid

Daniel Cassidy, *The Scholarship Book 2000: The Complete Guide to Private Sector Scholarships, Grants, and Loans for Undergraduates.* Prentice Hall Press, June 1999. Sixth edition.
Price: $31.00, ISBN: 0130207322.

The Scholarship Book 2000 contains listings of scholarships, grants, loans, fellowships, internships, and prizes available from governmental and institutional sources. Contents of this book are alphabetically arranged according to major field of study and name of award. Other chapters list 73 financial assistance publications and 387 national organizations that offer career guidance. Sample form letters for requesting applications and guidance tips on how to apply are also included.

Other Educational Resources

Educational Resources Information Center (ERIC)
3051 Moore Hall, Box 951521
University of California
Los Angeles, CA 90095-1521
(800) 832-8256
Web site: www.*accesseric.org*

Educational Resources Information Center is a service of the U.S. Department of Education that covers all fields in education and all academic disciplines. ERIC provides several references, which provide an overview of issues, programs, and research related to the education priorities established by the president and the secretary of the U.S. Department of Education.

Educational Testing Service (ETS)
Rosedale Road
Princeton, NJ 08541
(609) 921-9000
Web site: *www.ets.org*

Educational Testing Service provides a number of testing programs (e.g., SAT, GRE, GMAT) and services for admissions, selection, placement, and guidance for educational objectives as well as occupational licensing and certification.

Appendix C. Budget, Finance, and Tax Resources

Finance Resources

GE Center for Financial Learning
Web site: *www.financiallearning.com*

GE Center for Financial Learning educates adults on personal financial matters. A mix of experts covers topics such as retirement planning, estate planning, managing taxes, building a financial plan, investments, insurance, and other related subjects.

HSH Associates
1200 Route 23
Butler, NJ 07405
Web site: *www.hsh.com*
(800) 873-2837

HSH Associates is a large publisher of a variety of financial information, such as lenders and rates, loan rates index, statistical index, ARM indexes, and many more. One of HSH Associates' services is a program called *home plans*, which shows you how to finance your construction, how to avoid pitfalls, and how to locate the best resources to find out about mortgages, consumer loans, auto loans, home equity loans, and related subjects.

SDI Capital
Web site: *www.sdicapital.com*
(800) SDI-TEAM

SDI Capital helps you with every aspect of the leasing process. It designs programs in conjunction with equipment dealers and manufacturers to help create innovative solutions, such as healthcare equipment financing, healthcare practice acquisition financing, healthcare working capital, technology equipment financing, industrial equipment financing, and church financing.

Tax Resources

H&R Block Accountants Referral
Web site: *www.hrblock.com*

H&R Block is a chain of tax service firms that you will find in most cities. H&R Block will prepare your tax returns at a reasonable fee. On their Web site, you will find valuable information such as key dates for all taxpayers, information on tax law changes, tax tips, state tax information, and other related subjects.

Note: You will find other tax preparers in your area other than H&R Block.

Internal Revenue Service (IRS)
Web site: *www.irs.gov*
(800) 829-3676

The IRS publishes tax information to help individual taxpayers and business owners. You can visit an IRS office to pick up copies of IRS forms and publications, you can call the IRS to request forms and publications free of charge, or you can browse and download IRS forms and publications from the IRS Web site. You also can get interactive help with your taxes while you are online. Some IRS publications that small business owners may find helpful include IRS Publication 334, Tax Guide for Small Businesses, and Publication 910, Guide to Free Tax Services, which provides a listing and brief description of 100 IRS tax publications.

Tax Software

You can buy tax preparation programs at computer stores or through the Internet from Web sites such as *Buy.com*, *Amazon.com*, and *Barnesandnoble.com.*

- *TurboTax* (about $30) asks you simple questions tailored to your tax situation, automatically selects and completes the forms you need, and double checks your tax return.
- *TurboTax Home and Business* (about $69) is ideal for sole proprietorships and home businesses.
- *Quicken TurboTax Deluxe* (about $45) is the fastest, easiest, most complete way to calculate and file your taxes. TurboTax

interviews you, completes IRS-approved forms, and then either prints them for you or instantly files them electronically.

Yahoo Tax Center
Web site: *www.yahoo.com*

Yahoo's software can help you prepare and electronically file federal and state returns. You can file your taxes easily and quickly online. The software includes the following features: tax refund estimator, online tax filing, and tax preparation checklist. Tax tips include credits, deductions, family education, home, property, income/employment, and investments.

Investor Associations

American Association of Individual Investors (AAII)
625 N. Michigan Avenue
Chicago, IL 60611
Web site: *www.aaii.org*

American Association of Individual Investors assists individuals in becoming effective managers of their own assets. It also offers home-study courses on investment topics, sponsors seminars, publishes several journals, and provides an electronic bulletin board.

National Association of Investors Corporation (NAIC)
1515 E. Eleven Mile Road
Royal Oak, MI 48067
Web site: *www.better-investing.org*

National Association of Investors helps people set up investment clubs and monitors their performance. NAIC offers many unique products, services, and professional support to help members become informed investors. Most of NAIC's investment analysis forms and guides are easy to learn and use and provide a sound, proven method for investment analysis.

Books on Finance

Essentials of Business Budgeting (Worksmart)
Robert G. Finney, AMACOM, 1995
Price: $10.95. ISBN: 0814478360.

Essentials of Business Budgeting is concise and provides you with all the skills you need to participate in the budgeting process and turn it into a powerful decision-making tool.

Basic Budgeting and Money Management: A Guide for Taking Control of Your Spending
Tuttie Peetz, Systems Co., 1997
Price: $23.00, ISBN: 1562162500

Basic Budgeting and Money Management covers many aspects of money management, such as budgeting, financial goals, and savings.

Making the Most of Your Money
Jane Bryant Quinn, Simon and Schuster, 1997
Price: $30.00, ISBN: 0684811766

Making the Most of Your Money helps you see where you stand on money matters and explains basic money management techniques. It includes helpful explanations about insurance needs, home ownership, college funding, investment planning, and retirement planning.

Appendix D. Business and Employment Resources

Business Associations

Association for Enterprise Opportunity (AEO)
353 Folsom Street
San Francisco, CA 94105
(510) 495-6945; (510) 495-7025 (fax)

Association for Enterprise Opportunity (AEO) provides its members with a forum and a voice to promote enterprise opportunity for people and communities that have limited access to economic resources.

Chamber of Commerce of the United States
1615 H St. NW
Washington, DC 20062
(202) 659-6000

Chamber of Commerce of the United States is a major advocate for business, particularly small businesses. It publishes *Nation's Business* and other magazines. It has 2,800 state and local affiliates.

Center for Community Futures (CCF)
P.O. Box 5309, Elmwood Station
Berkeley, CA 94705
(510) 540-1928

Center for Community Futures assists both nonprofit agencies and individuals in starting profit-making businesses.

National Business Association (NBA)
5025 Arapaho, Suite 515
Dallas, TX 75248
(800) 456-0440

National Business Association promotes the growth of small businesses by helping members obtain government loans; offers insurance and software in conjunction with the U.S. Small Business Administration; and sponsors seminars and trade shows.

National Federation of Independent Businesses (NFIB)
150 W. 20th Avenue
San Mateo, CA 9440
(415) 341-7441

National Federation of Independent Businesses represents small and independent businesses. NFIB provides a variety of services from lobbying to surveys on economic trends.

National Small Business Benefits Association (NSBBA)
2244 N. Grand Avenue East
Springfield, IL 62702
(217) 753-2558

National Small Business Benefits Association offers businesses with fewer than two hundred employees discounts on group dental and life insurance, travel programs, fax equipment, office supplies, and cellular phone service. NSBBA also provides management consulting, accounting services, and owner-to-owner networking.

Employment Associations

American Counseling Association (ACA)
5999 Stevenson Avenue
Alexandria, VA 22304
(703) 823-9800

American Counseling Association provides human development and counseling professionals in schools, colleges, government, and industry. The association maintains a library and publishes many journals.

College Placement Council (CPC)
62 Highland Avenue
Bethlehem, PA 18017
(215) 868-1421

College Placement Council issues publications for recent college graduates, including salary surveys, guides to career planning, and directories of employment opportunities.

Online Services for Job Seekers

Many online systems help job seekers by listing job openings and, for a fee, posting résumés for employers to view. Some states also offer free online listings of job vacancies through local state employment offices, community colleges, and high schools.

America Online
Web site: *www.aol.com*

America Online (AOL) contains a Career Center with many tools for job seekers, including résumé templates and a collection of cover letters that can be downloaded. There are monthly articles on career guidance, an occupational profiles database with 700 occupations, and a Federal Employment Service that describes agencies and types of jobs with the government.

CompuServe
Web site: *www.compuserve.com*

CompuServe has many industry-specific bulletin boards that often contain listings of job openings, plus the College Recruitment Database, which posts résumés of recent college graduates.

CareerBuilder
Web site: *www.careerbuilder.com*

CareerBuilder is the leading provider of targeted interactive recruiting on the Web. Job seekers have the ability to access more than three million career postings—practically every job on the Internet as well as insightful career advice. In addition, "my CareerBuilder" simplifies and personalizes the job-hunting process by providing job seekers the tools for a quality job search.

Futurestep
Web site: *www.futurestep.com*

Futurestep provides articles on industry and hiring trends, career management advice, and enables interviews with recruiters. It offers job seekers the opportunity to "E-mail a Recruiter" to discuss a personal career question they may be facing. It also offers live discussion events where visitors can pose questions to recruiters and other guest speakers.

HotJobs.com
Web site: *www.hotjobs.com*

HotJobs.com is a leading Internet-based recruiting solutions company. Its suite of services leverages the Internet to provide a direct exchange of information between job seekers and employers. These services were developed based on the needs of job seekers and employers. By solving many of the problems associated with traditional recruiting methods, HotJobs.com allows employers to more effectively manage recruiting methods to save time and money.

Job Interview Resources (JIR)
Web site: *www.job-interview.net*

Job Interview Resources provides information about different types of questions. For job interview questions based on the job or profession, click on "Interview Tips by Job." JIR also gives access to topics such as tough job interview questions, job interview guides, mock job interviews, sample job interview questions, job interview tips, and interview success stories.

Monster.com
Web site: *www.monster.com*

Monster.com is a job search engine that provides thousands of job postings, a career center that offers career advice, information, and resources, and a salary center where job seekers can get salary scales on specific jobs and other job-related subjects.

Employment Agencies

Following is a sample list of agencies that recruit people for skilled, semiskilled, domestic services, professional, and executive/managerial positions.

AMERICA AT WORK
Web site: *www.americaatwork.com*

AMERICA AT WORK specializes in recruitment and placement of bilingual/bicultural professionals.

JobsInSports.com
Web site: *www.jobsinsports.com*

JobsInSports.com is an Internet-based employment service dedicated to helping people find jobs in the highly competitive sports marketplace.

The Search Connection
Web site: *www.thesearchconnection.com*

The Search Connection specializes in the executive search for professionals from high technology sectors.

A-Plus Domestic Services, Inc.
9201 Wilshire Blvd., Suite 105
Beverly Hills, CA 90210
(310) 247-9881; (310) 247-9895 (fax)
Web site: *www.aplus.dom.com*

A-Plus Domestic Services Incorporated is a nationwide domestic employment agency that offers qualified and reliable staffing at reasonable rates, which are paid by the employer. Recruitment includes jobs for nannies, chauffeurs, day workers, housekeepers, chefs, personal assistants, governesses, caregivers, maids, cooks, nurse assistants, waiters, butlers, baby nurses, and many more.

Chris Hamilton & Associates, LLC
P.O. Box 1173
Irmo, SC 29063
(803) 749-8880; (803) 749-8881 (fax)
Web site: *www.chrishamiltonandassoc.com*

Chris Hamilton and Associates, LLC, specializes in placing restaurant professionals with the country's best restaurants. This agency can place people in jobs in their local area or elsewhere in America.

Analytic Recruiting, Inc.
12 East 41st Street, 9th Floor
New York, NY 10017
(212) 545-8511; (212) 545-8520 (fax)
Web site: *www.analyticrecruiting.com*

Analytic Recruiting specializes in recruitment of people with strong analytical skills. Its practice is nationwide and covers all major business areas, including finance, marketing, operations, manufacturing, planning, and systems. Analytic recruits for positions that emphasize use of advanced quantitative/modeling techniques and technology in business decision making.

Careers, Ltd.
(303) 832-5200; (303) 832-9365 (fax)
Web site: www.careersltd.com

Careers, Ltd., places qualified professionals with a wide variety of corporate clients. Its clients include Fortune 500 companies within every industry. Careers, Ltd. has a large privately held database containing the top 10 percent of professionals in the industry. The agency specializes in jobs in information technology, accounting, engineering, insurance services, office support, and sales.

Business and Career Books

Business

Ironing It Out: Seven Simple Steps to Resolving Conflict
Charles P. Lickson, Crisp Publications, 1996
Price: $14.95, ISBN: 1560523794
95 First Street, Los Altos, CA 94022
(415) 949-4888; (415) 949-1610 (fax)

Ironing It Out: Seven Simple Steps to Resolving Conflict combines wisdom, wit, and patience with practical application and theory.

Sustaining the Family Business: An Insider's Guide to Managing Across Generations
Marshall B. Paisner, Perseus Press, 1999
Price: $26.00, ISBN: 0738201146

Sustaining the Family Business is a practical guide to successful management—today and tomorrow—of the family business.

Job Interviews

The Complete Q and A Job Interview Book
Jeffrey G. Allen, John Wiley & Sons, 1997
Price: $14.95, ISBN: 0471180947

The Complete Q & A Job Interview Book is a practical, hands-on guide to putting your best foot forward in job interviews.

60 Seconds and You're Hired!
Robin Ryan, Penguin USA, 2000
Price: $10.95, ISBN: 0140289038

60 Seconds and You're Hired! provides concise advice and easy-to-learn techniques for mastering the interview process and landing a great job. This book presents strategies based on current hiring trends, including how to give the best answers to the interviewer's questions and communicate that you are the right person for the job, and other interviewing techniques.

Career Exploration

Career Information Center
Macmillan Library Reference. 1999. 13 volumes. Seventh edition.
Price: $278.00, ISBN: 002864915X

Career Information Center is a set of reference books providing information about jobs requiring no specialized training, some specialized training or experience, and advanced training and experience. Extensive further reading and resource lists note titles for each career.

The Encyclopedia of Careers and Vocational Guidance
William Hopke, Ferguson Publishing, 1999
Price: $159.95, ISBN: 0894342908

The Encyclopedia of Careers and Vocational Guidance is similar to but broader in scope than the Occupational Outlook Handbook. Volume 1 profiles various industries; Volume 2 gives overviews of professional careers; Volume 3, general and special careers, and Volume 4, technical careers.

Career Success

Going to the Top: A Road Map for Success from America's Leading Women Executives
Carol A. Gallagher, Viking Press, 2000
Price: $24.95, ISBN: 0670891517

Going to the Top is an authoritative guide to climbing the corporate ladder based on lessons learned from 200 women executives who made it to the top.

Job Savvy: How to Be a Success at Work
La Verne L. Ludden, Trade Paperback, 1997
Price: $12.95, ISBN: 1563703041

Job Savvy: How to Be a Success at Work gives advice for new employees on how to avoid mistakes and improve performance and satisfaction, turning a new job into a rewarding career.

What's Holding You Back? 8 Critical Choices for Women's Success
Linda S. Austin, Basic Books, 2000
Price: $25.00, ISBN: 0465032621

What's Holding You Back? provides information on what women need to break through the glass ceiling.

Samples of U.S. Standard Résumés

Résumés are important tools for seeking jobs. They give headhunters, employment agencies, and hiring managers a big picture of what you are all about—your educational background, employment history, personal attributes—and other key information needed to determine whether you have the right qualifications for a particular job.

Just like the old saying "first impressions last," when you appear for a job interview, your résumé conveys the first impression, but in written form. You should prepare your résumé carefully and neatly. If you do not know how to prepare one, you can always find "résumé-creating companies" that can prepare a professional-looking document for you at minimal cost. If you want to create your own résumé, you can use software that does it easily for you or you can purchase a "how to prepare your résumé" book that will guide you in preparing one.

Remember, the presentation of your résumé is important (e.g., use a readable font), especially now that you can send résumés through the Internet or by fax. It used to be that you could only send résumés through the mail, so you had to use an appropriate texture and color of paper on which to print. But now with advancing technology, most employers give you the flexibility to send your résumé either by fax or electronically via e-mail.

In the next few pages, you will see some examples that may be helpful to you.

Sample 1 - Résumé

Home: (703) 555-1212 John Doe
Office: (703) 555-2222 208 Deere Street
Leesburg, VA 20000

SENIOR CONSULTANT with diversified international experience, particularly in human resources, as an advisor to private and public sector executives and staff members.

Background includes:

- Analyzing issues, determining objectives, devising strategies, and proposing actions
- Formulating policies to achieve organizational objectives and optimal use of human resources
- Integrating human resource planning with business planning
- Planning and organizing personnel and administrative support for overseas projects
- Developing virtual teams and maintaining effective workgroup relations.

Personal attributes include: Analytical and thoughtful in approach to problems. Energetic and dedicated. Skillful in balancing organizational requirements and individual needs. Organized, articulate, and precise. Professional and dependable in achieving the desired results.

AREAS OF SPECIAL COMPETENCE

- Organizational Development
- Outplacement
- Performance Planning and Review
- Career Counseling
- Organizational Problem Solving
- Spouse Relocation

These skills were developed in the private sector with:

- Sin Poh Amalgamated, Inc., rising from management trainee to Director–Organization and Executive Development (Singapore)
- Think Tank Career Planning, Vice President;
  and in the public sector with:
  U.S. Embassy as Assistant Director of Administration (Korea)

EDUCATION

BA and MBA, University of Korea.

Sample 2 - Résumé

Juanita T. Gomez
20 High Street
Atlanta, Georgia 30313
Phone: (404) 555-2222

OBJECTIVE
Top-level responsibility for international operations of technology-based company in the pharmaceutical industry.

BACKGROUND SUMMARY
Fifteen years' successful experience in building pharmaceutical business in Latin America, with a strong record of achieving results in difficult regulatory and economic environments; development of leadership and management talent; and meeting or exceeding investment goals.

CAREER HISTORY AND ACCOMPLISHMENTS
SAN MIGUEL CORPORATION
Managing Director, Venezuela (1985-1990)

- Responsible for managing Venezuelan distribution subsidiary with full support from programming design staff.
- Increased Venezuelan sales by 40% and profit contribution by 60% in three years with her appointment of a more effective General Manager who focused on overhead cost reductions of daily operations.
- Established successful joint venture company in Brazil, which provided one of the first expansions into that important market. This was based on cautious investments in plant and reduction of risks of the overall venture.

General Manager, Brazil (1990-2000)

- Responsible for operations in distributor markets in Chile, Peru, and Puerto Rico to ensure the successful marketing of two new products.
- Negotiated new and revised distributorship in Chile and Peru, which provided much improved control of marketing efforts.
- Developed a central Medical and Sales/Marketing Services operation to service distributor markets in other Latin American countries. This provided the vehicle for successful, coordinated marketing efforts in a considerable number of smaller markets, with dramatic growth in revenue and market shares.

EDUCATIONAL BACKGROUND
MA, International Affairs, London School of Economics
BA, Information Technology, University of Venezuela
Fluent in Spanish, conversant in English

Sample 3 - Response to an Advertisement

December 1, 2000

Mr. Donald Rooney
Manager, Human Resources
Shoreline Industries
100 Seaside Avenue
New York, NY 10234

Dear Mr. Rooney:

This is in reply to your advertisement for an Accounting Representative, which appeared in the Sunday New York Inquirer on November 26, 2000. As the following comparison shows, my experience and background match this position's requirements.

Your Requirements	**My Qualifications**
Three to five years accounting experience	Five years in-depth accounting experience. Results achieved in reducing costs and improving inventory control for three years; responsible for administration of staff of five.
Strong communication skills	Proven excellence in ongoing oral skills and written communications with clients and staff. Developed and presented operational procedures and accounting manuals.
Knowledge of complex accounting systems	Extensive knowledge of processing in complex accounting systems. This includes generating input and analyzing output, and updating existing systems to provide greater operational flexibility.

I would like an opportunity to discuss the position with you in person, and will call you in a few days for a meeting. You may also call me at home or leave a message at 1-800-555-5555.

Sincerely,

Mai T. Lee
20000 T. Lee Court
Ashburn, VA 20147

Appendix E. Holidays and Festivals

America observes legal or federal holidays and allows you to observe your own religious holidays. Everyone in America, including the government, observes official holidays such as July 4th, which is Independence Day. Religious holidays are unique and are observed by each ethnic group separately.

In addition to holidays, each ethnic group celebrates other events. A popular example is the Mardi Gras in New Orleans, which occurs on Fat Tuesday, the last day before Lent.

Many of the holidays, events, or festivals in America increasingly reflect the multi-ethnic heritage of immigrants. As in ethnic holidays such as the Chinese New Year, non-Chinese people also partake of these festivities because they are fun.

Travel guides and books provide a comprehensive list of holidays and events.

Legal and Federal Holidays

New Year's Day—January 1. One of the rare days in America when almost everything shuts down. New Year's Day has its origin in Roman times, when sacrifices were offered to Janus, the two-faced Roman god who looked back on the past and forward to the future.

Martin Luther King Jr.'s Birthday—Celebrated on the third Monday of January. An important day to reflect upon the actions and values of the preeminent civil rights leader.

Presidents Day—Third Monday of February. Originally meant to honor our first president, George Washington, born February 22, 1732, the holiday now also honors our sixteenth president, Abraham Lincoln, whose birthdate, February 12, 1809, had been commemorated as a separate holiday. Parades occur in some cities to rouse the patriotic spirit. Department stores almost everywhere have huge "Presidents Day Sales" as store owners increasingly transform the date into an opportunity to empty their shelves of excess winter inventories and promote the sale of spring clothes.

Memorial Day—Last Monday in May. This holiday honors the men and women who lost their lives serving in all wars. Special ceremonies are held in Washington, DC, and at national cemeteries around the country. Memorial Day is also celebrated with parades throughout America. The holiday has also been known as Decoration Day, when the graves of servicemen and women are decorated with flowers.

Independence Day—July 4. This is when the United States celebrates the anniversary of its freedom from British colonialism, with parades in almost every village, town, and city followed by picnics, cookouts, and fireworks displays of all kinds.

Labor Day—First Monday in September. It is the day to honor the workers of America and their labor, which has made the American way of life the envy of the rest of the world.

Columbus Day—Second Monday in October. Columbus Day is celebrated to honor the discovery of America in 1492, but for some people it is a sad reminder that the arrival of Europeans marked the beginning of the end for the Native Americans. Occurring at the height of the fall colors in northern states, Columbus Day is the last three-day weekend before winter.

Veterans Day—November 11, formerly known as Armistice Day. This federal holiday was established in 1926 to commemorate the signing in 1918 of the armistice ending World War I. On June 1, 1954, the name was changed to Veterans Day to honor all brave men and women who were called upon to serve their country.

Thanksgiving—Fourth Thursday of November. It commemorates the time when the first immigrants broke bread with the Native Americans, who helped them survive in the alien new world. Family and friends get together for a traditional meal—typically turkey with stuffing, cranberries, mashed potatoes, yams, and a variety of pies. Thanksgiving also kicks off the official holiday shopping season.

Religious Holidays

Passover (Pesach)—A week in late March or in April, in accordance with the Jewish calendar. The Feast of the Passover, also called the Feast of Unleavened Bread, commemorates the escape of the Jews from Egypt. As they fled, they ate unleavened bread, and from that time, observant Jews have allowed no leavening in their houses during Passover, bread being replaced by matzoh.

Easter—First Sunday after the first full moon that occurs on or after March 21. This is a Christian holiday celebrating the resurrection of Jesus Christ. Religious ceremonies vary from community to community. Easter "parades" occur in some towns and cities, such as New York, on Easter Sunday as people celebrate spring and the wearing of new clothes. Many schools and colleges have "spring break," usually a week, to coincide with this time.

Yom Kippur—Mid-September or early October. Called the Day of Atonement, Yom Kippur marks the end of ten days of repentance that begin with Rosh Hashanah, the Jewish New Year. It is described as a "Sabbath of rest," and synagogue services begin at sundown the next day.

Hanukkah—Begins in late November or in December. Also spelled Chanukah, this is the eight-day Festival of Lights celebrated by people of Jewish faith. This holiday honors a historical event in which a small band of Jews triumphed in a struggle to preserve their heritage. Hanukkah means rededication, and the symbols and rituals of the holiday demonstrate an annual renewal of Jewish faith and practices.

Ramadan—The first day of Ramadan is usually during the second week of December. The actual date changes according to the Islamic calendar. The first day marks the beginning of a month-long fast that all Muslims must keep during the daylight hours. It commemorates the first revelation of the Qur'an.

Christmas—December 25. The traditional date of December 25 was set in 375 AD for the Western Church, but the Eastern Church celebrates Christmas on January 6. On this day, people exchange gifts with family and friends, and celebrate the birth of Jesus.

Festivals

New Year's Eve—December 31. This is the last hurrah in preparation for the New Year, with much eating, drinking, and merriment. Everyone looks forward with excitement to the opportunities the New Year will bring.

Chinese New Year—The first day of the Chinese lunar calendar, usually in mid-February. This is probably the largest Chinese celebration. Each year is named after one of the twelve animals according to the Chinese Zodiac. Customs include paying off debts, purchasing new clothes, thoroughly cleaning the house, enjoying sumptuous family feasts, offering sacrifices to the gods, and giving friends and relatives red envelopes containing "lucky money."

St. Patrick's Day—March 17. St. Patrick's Day is when many people drink green beer for the first and probably only time in their lives. Why green? Green is the traditional color of Ireland, like the color of the Irish flag and the shamrock. Parades are staged in cities such as New York, Boston, and other heavily Irish-populated areas. The best place to be is in any Irish bar. Old-fashioned restaurants serve the evening's special—corned beef with boiled potatoes and cabbage—at a discount price. Although St. Patrick's Day may be the largest ethnic spectacle in the United States, in Ireland it is a religious day accompanied by church ceremonies, much like Christmas and Easter.

Mardi Gras—Celebrated in New Orleans and elsewhere on the last day before Lent known as Fat Tuesday or Shrove Tuesday. The date varies depending on when Lent occurs. Lent is for Christians a time of penitence, lasting from Ash Wednesday until Easter Sunday. The observance of a "carnival" (Mardi Gras) before the Lenten period is not new. It originated in the middle of the second century in Rome before the Fast of the Forty Days during which time participants delivered themselves up to voluntary madness, put on masks, clothed themselves like specters, gave themselves up to Bacchus and Venus, and considered all pleasures allowable.

Cinco de Mayo—May 5. This is the day when cities with large Hispanic or Latino populations—San Antonio and other cities in Texas, Los Angeles, Miami, and San Francisco—recall the Mexican victory over the French when the French sent troops to Mexico in

1862. The celebration includes parades, costumes, dancing, music, food, and other expressions of Hispanic pride.

Chicago Blues Festival—Takes place on the second weekend of June. It celebrates the history and tradition of the music, while introducing listeners to the next generation of blues artists.

Aloha Festival—September 22 through October 29. This is Hawaii's largest festival and the only statewide celebration in the United States consisting of a cultural celebration of music, dance, and history intended to preserve unique traditions. The Aloha Festival has grown over the past 50 years to include 300 events on six islands (Oahu, Hawaii, Molokai, Lanai, Kauai, and Maui), now spanning a two-month period. The Aloha Festival has become a celebration of Pacific, Asian, and Western cultural influences, from the Japanese Bon Dance to the traditional hula.

Halloween or All Hallow's Eve—October 31. Events include costume parties and trick-or-treating, where children dress up in costumes and go door-to-door and receive candies, fruits, or coins at the houses they visit. Parents usually accompany the younger children, and the older kids usually go with their friends. Many communities now stipulate certain hours on the preceding Sunday afternoon for trick-or-treating.

Kwanzaa—Begins December 26. Kwanzaa means "first fruits" in Swahili, an African language. This seven-day African-American festival celebrates seven virtues, including responsibility and cooperation.

Other Important Dates

Valentine's Day—February 14. It is a modern celebration, which usually involves sending cards, chocolates, or flowers to special people you love, such as spouses, sweethearts, family members, or close friends.

Mother's Day—Second Sunday in May. Mother's Day is celebrated in many different countries, though not all celebrate it on the same date as America. The days and the ways may be different, yet the idea is still the same—to honor mothers in some special way.

Father's Day—Third Sunday of June. Father's Day began in the United States, but no one knows quite where and when. In 1924, President Calvin Coolidge supported the idea of a national Father's Day. Finally, in 1966 President Lyndon Johnson signed a presidential proclamation setting the current date.

Notes

Part I: Working and Living in the United States

1. *Figuring Foreigners Out.* Craig Storti, Intercultural Press, Inc., 1999. Price: $19.95, ISBN: 1877864706.

2. *We Are All Multiculturalists Now.* Nathan Glazer, Harvard University Press, 1998. Price: $12.95, ISBN: 067494836X.

3. *The Fiske Guide to Colleges.* Edward B. Fiske, Three Rivers Press, 2001. Price: $21.00, ISBN: 0-8129-3172-6.

4. "More High-Tech Worker Visas Sought," *H-1B Visa Quota News,* March 16, 2000.

5. "In Short Supply: Teachers Join Special Visa List," *Washington Post,* December 24, 1999.

6. Retirement plan options. Web site: *www.taxes.yahoo.com.*

7. *More Wealth Without Risks.* Charles J. Givens, Pocket Books, 1995. Price: $16.00, ISBN: 0-6716-9403-0.

8. "Support from a High-Tech Family," *Washington Business Magazine,* November 15, 1999.

Part II: Achieving Success

9. "The Three Levels of the Glass Ceiling: Sorcerer's Apprentice Through the Looking Glass," *www.cyberwerks.com,* July 5, 2000.

10. "Glass Ceiling Is Cracked, Not Broken, for Women in Technology," by Anne Mulcahy, *Rochester Democrat and Chronicle*, August 1999.

11. *Los Angeles Times*, May 18, 2000.

Part III: Visiting the United States the First Time

12. Information that appears on the Non-Immigrant Visas table was obtained from the Web site *www.grasmick.com.* Information can

also be found in *Immigrating to the USA,* Dan P. Danilov, Bellingham, WA: Self-Counsel Press Legal Series, 1999.

13. Information that appears on the Immigrant Visas table was obtained from the Web sites *www.grasmick.com* and *www.foreignborn.com.*

14. Information on Key Immigration Laws can be accessed from Web site *www.grasmick.com.*

15. Tipping Standards in America. Web sites: *www.tipping.org* and *www.channel2000.com.*

Epilogue

16. *Migrations and Cultures: A World View.* Thomas Sowell, HarperCollins, 1997. Price: $20.00, ISBN: 0465045898.

Index

Contributors

Christina Bonnell is from Trinidad and Tobago. She has lived in America for the past thirty-five years, loving every minute of it. Before she became a realtor, she worked at the World Bank in Washington, DC, with her latest job in the personnel department.

In 1967, Christina took advanced courses in commercial law and commercial management at Mankato Commercial College in Minnesota. These courses helped her embark on a new endeavor. Becoming a realtor in 1988, she is now a multimillion-dollar real estate agent in Maryland and Washington, DC. Life is good for her as a single person because many nephews and nieces surround her. At some point, she plans to return to her home country.

Louis Cheng, originally from Taiwan, has lived in America for twenty years. Even though his friends and most of his customers say to him that he is a successful businessman, he is more content to say that he is proud of having created two well-recognized business establishments from almost nothing.

Louis has been working very hard all these years. His mind is always set on how to improve his operations to exceed his goals. He is not afraid to take risks because he has confidence in his instincts and decisions. He accepts his competitors as a challenge to his own ability to perform and to react. And he believes that only the better business operations will survive.

Mike Ghanna was born in Jerusalem, Israel, and has lived in the United States for twelve years. He arrived in New York City in 1989, but chose to live in the Washington, DC area, specifically northern Virginia. Mike worked for relatives in earlier years, in a deli shop, in the transportation (limo) business, and later in a restaurant business.

When Mike gained enough experience and saved enough money, he decided he wanted to be his own boss. He had learned enough by working in the transportation business to know when it was time for him to spread his wings and start his own limousine business. He owns two limousines and is enjoying the flexibility of owning his own business. Mike is married to a fellow Israeli and has two young children, both born in the United States.

Maria Jaramillo originally came from Chihuahua, Mexico. Her parents were born in the United States, but they moved back to Mexico when they had children. The family returned to America and settled in El Paso, Texas, when Maria was nine. To process the legalization of the children's papers, the family moved to Juarez. The process took a year. Maria married a native-born American from Belen, New Mexico. They have four children.

Before her retirement in January 2000, Maria taught physical education for four years at a private school, the Sacred Heart Elementary School in Nogales, Arizona. Previously, she worked as manager in retail stores and as a substitute teacher in Fullerton, California.

Georg Hirsch is a Washington, DC-based freelance correspondent for the German Public Radio Network. His special field is classical music, and he also covers some jazz. He came to Washington in 1991 when the Voice of America (VOA) opened a German language service, and set out on his own when VOA closed that service in 1993. Georg completed his undergraduate work in music and physical education in Hamburg, Germany. In 1987, he started his master's degree in journalism at the University of Iowa, Iowa City, where he graduated in 1989. Georg lives alone. He is a permanent resident based on outstanding ability in his area of expertise.

Dave Lang came with his family as refugees from Vietnam in 1975. He is from an upper-class family in Saigon. Living there, he studied two foreign languages, English and French, in preparation for emigrating. Immigration officers processed the Langs' papers at the military base in Guam. The process took a month. With all paperwork done, social security cards and Form I-94 in hand, Dave and his family were transferred to Arkansas' Fort Mead refugee camp, where sponsors chose refugees through the Christian Lutheran Church. The refugees worked in the facility, and later Dave and his siblings worked at restaurants and hotels in the area.

Sponsors from Simaron, Kansas provided the family with a house for a year. The sponsors also paid for food until Dave found work.

Parishioners provided clothing and necessities for the house. Dave prospered in retail jobs, and after moving from state to state for better economic opportunities, he moved to Virginia when a friend convinced him that it was the place to be. Dave improved his already excellent people skills, which gave him the push in the right direction to be successful as owner of a nail salon and to eventually open a second nail salon in the same area. He is married to a fellow Vietnamese and has an American-born daughter.

Ellen Dimaano Latham was born in Batangas, Philippines. She obtained a bachelor of arts in English from the University of the East. She worked for the Philippine National Library and later the United Nations office in Manila. Being adventurous, she emigrated to Canada and worked as an executive secretary in Vancouver and later Toronto.

After spending five years in Canada, Ellen moved to America and found work as an executive secretary, first with the Pan American Health Organization (now called World Health Organization) and then the International Monetary Fund (IMF). After marriage, she left the IMF to raise her family. Now that her children are grown, she works part-time as an executive secretary and lives with her husband in Northern Virginia.

Elena Minnitti grew up in a family that valued education. Her parents, who were not wealthy, often told her and her siblings that the only thing of real value they could leave to them was a good education—something that nobody could ever take away. After obtaining her bachelor of science degree in chemistry at the University of the Philippines, Elena left in 1989 to take her Ph.D. in chemistry at the State University of New York. This made all the difference in her life. Her education has assured her of a good job.

Elena is now a research scientist at one of the top pharmaceutical companies in the world. Her career in developing drugs to fight cancer and AIDS makes her feel she has something significant to contribute to mankind. She has met people from all over the world, and this opportunity has given her a deeper insight into people and into life. All her experiences in America have been enriching and fulfilling. She wishes more people could have the same opportunities.

Bella Morin is originally from the Philippines. Like Ellen, Bella first migrated to Canada in the late 1960s before moving to America in 1971. She works at the International Finance Corporation, an affiliate of the World Bank based in Washington, DC. Married to a native-born American and with two college-aged daughters, she and her husband plan to live permanently in America. Having already lived for twenty-eight years in America, Bella considers this country her home. Future plans include retirement to a warmer area like Southern California.

Chung K. Pak, a South Korean, became a naturalized U.S. citizen in 1976. Chung is highly educated with a degree in chemical engineering from Auburn University and a law degree from Catholic University Law School in Washington, DC. He is currently working as an administrative patent judge at the Board of Patent Appeals and Interferences, United States Patent and Trademark Office.

Very active in his community, Chung helps ethnic groups with immigration, social, and legal issues. With a full-time, demanding job as a patent judge, he does not find it easy to make time for his extracurricular activities, but he loves to help his fellow Koreans and other ethnic groups integrate successfully into American society.

Sam Quaye is from Ghana and came to America to study. However, Sam did not follow through with his original intention to go to medical school. Instead, he became a cab driver and now owns his own cab. The flexibility of owning his business allows him to spend time with his young children.

Nilofer Qureshi grew up in Pakistan and completed her bachelor of science in economics at the University of Karachi. She met and married a fellow Pakistani who was already a naturalized U.S. citizen and joined him in December 1981 in Milford, Connecticut.

In the twenty years that Nilofer has been in America, she worked for commercial banks in New York and Connecticut until September 1986, when she joined Xerox Corporation. Nilofer held a variety of jobs for the last fourteen years and currently works full-time as an administrative training developer. Her outside activities include reading, photography, travel, and cooking. Nilofer and her husband plan to stay in America permanently.

Bharat Sahay was armed with a bachelor of science degree in electrical engineering from Bihar Institute of Technology in Bihar, India, before migrating to America. In addition to this degree, he was a graduate research fellow in electrical engineering (power systems) at the Indian Institute of Technology, Kampur, India.

Bharat has earned a master's degree from City College of New York and majored in electrical engineering, specializing in digital systems (computer architecture and digital signal processing). He also earned an MBA from Rochester Institute of Technology. As a systems design specialist in a large corporation, he is in a career he thoroughly enjoys. Although he visits his home country often with his wife and children, America is now home for him and his family.

Ravi Sahay came to America in 1971 to study and completed an advanced degree in engineering at the City College of New York. He also completed an MBA at the University of Rochester. Proud of his origin as an East Indian and his success as a naturalized U.S. citizen, Ravi now owns his own consulting practice in San Diego. His wife is in the same profession. He considers America home but visits India often so that his children can understand their roots.

Julio Sasaki was born in Peru, although he is of Japanese ancestry. He came to America in the late 1970s to study and complete his doctoral degree in industrial psychology at Bowling Green University in Ohio. Since the time that he contributed to this book, Julio has received a promotion from Marketing Manager to Manager of Management Information Systems. He is currently arranging to relocate his family (wife, and two young sons) to Rochester, New York.

Liklik G. Schroeder originally came from the Philippines in 1982 through the family preference visa program. Her mother sponsored her together with several siblings who had been anticipating coming to America after years of waiting patiently. Armed with a BS degree in business administration from the University of the East in the Philippines, Liklik found jobs in commercial banks both in the Philippines and in America. While she was working in a bank in San Francisco, the bank merged with another, which got her transferred to Sacramento, where she met her American-born husband, Gene.

Liklik and her husband are in a vacuum cleaner business called Rainbow. It is a thriving business and company sales have extended outside of the Sacramento area, and even outside of the United States. With a hundred employees who are motivated and committed to their sales jobs, Liklik and her husband make it a point to reward them with travels to different places such as Hawaii and Las Vegas. The main reason for the success of their business is Liklik's excellent interpersonal skills, which are a natural part of her vibrant personality.

Lina Shoobridge is British but of Greek parentage. Although she has lived in America for most of her adult life, she remains on a G-4 or international visa and has not attempted to apply for a green card so that she can reap the many benefits that her organization offers, such as tax-exempt income. She came to America in 1976 at age eighteen and worked for the World Bank for twelve years. She got married twice, both times to British citizens.

Lina has worked for the International Monetary Fund (IMF) since 1993. Her current husband is on a work permit under her G-4 visa, which was arranged by the State Department and processed through IMF's Legal Department. Lina lives with her husband and two young children.

Evelyn Shu is a happily married professional woman with two young children. Hong Kong is her country of origin. When she migrated to America, she had to live in Los Angeles because she was a student at Pasadena City College and UCLA, from which she graduated with a bachelor of arts degree in communication studies. She eventually married a man who lives in Los Angeles and whose family lives in the same area.

In a way, Evelyn never had the choice to move to another state because Chinese families are close-knit. She is happy to be in America and has achieved the goals she set for herself—marriage, children, and a fulfilling career—as an administrative training developer. Her mom often visits, and spending time with her family makes her very happy.

William (Bill) Skea grew up in a family that had little money. Without television or an automobile, they resorted to reading and games for stimulation, growth, and happiness. He was the only person from his area in the U.K. who attended the university. Bill obtained a bachelor of science honors degree in nuclear physics from the University of Manchester, Institute of Science and Technology. He learned that it is not the university degree that is important, but the training of the mind to reason, think, and meet challenges. He is currently involved in developing educational programs for the employees at Xerox Corporation.

Nora Szeto migrated from Hong Kong in 1986. Carrying her green card visa, she arrived at Hawaii, her port of entry, before proceeding to Maryland. She decided to live in Maryland, because a high school classmate lived there—the only person she knew at that time who was willing to help her out a little in getting settled in this country. Nora became a naturalized U.S. citizen in 1992.

Although Nora's main purpose in coming to America was to study, she did not register at the University of Maryland because she arrived in the middle of a semester. She decided to take a job first to save some money and enrolled one semester later. Nora has been in a variety of jobs in evaluation, research, and computer programming—the areas she loves.

Henry Tse is from Hong Kong. He completed high school but did not continue his education in America even with the prodding of his mother and sister. He is happy working as a waiter in a Chinese restaurant with the hope of saving as much as he can so that he can eventually go back to his homeland and start his own business.

Gabrielle Wittner is a twenty-year-old au pair from Switzerland. She came to America not only to work but also to see what the country is all about. She finds being away from her home country a humbling experience and is looking forward to returning to Switzerland a year older and wiser and ready to take on a more challenging task as a pharmaceutical assistant.

About the Author

Leticia (Letty) Gallares-Japzon came to America from the Philippines in 1971 and has lived in the Washington, DC area since. She has an MA in education and human development from George Washington University and an MA in human resource management from Marymount University.

Letty currently works as an independent management consultant and freelance writer. She has worked as a strategy and benchmarking manager at Xerox Corporation and has held positions in instructional design and development at both Xerox and the World Bank. Letty lives in Ashburn, Virginia, with her husband, Eddie.

About TeamCom

TeamCom is a customer-focused publishing company that combines the best of traditional print publishing with new media, such as e-books and the Internet. Our mission is to deliver high-quality books, Web content and related products to help people improve and enrich their lives.

For more information call 301-847-7600 or visit TeamComBooks.com